DEFINING DRESS

MANCHESTER
UNIVERSITY PRESS

STUDIES IN
DESIGN
AND
MATERIAL
CULTURE

general editor:
CHRISTOPHER BREWARD

Defining dress

DRESS AS OBJECT, MEANING AND IDENTITY

*edited by Amy de la Haye
and Elizabeth Wilson*

Manchester University Press

Manchester and New York

distributed exclusively in the USA by St. Martin's Press

Published by Manchester University Press
Oxford Road, Manchester M13 9NR, UK
and Room 400, 175 Fifth Avenue, New York, NY 10010, USA
http://www.man.ac.uk/mup

Distributed exclusively in the USA by
St. Martin's Press, Inc., 175 Fifth Avenue, New York,
NY 10010, USA

Distributed exclusively in Canada by
UBC Press, University of British Columbia, 6344 Memorial Road,
Vancouver, BC, Canada V6T 1Z2

British Library Cataloguing-in-Publication Data
A catalogue record for this book is available from the British Library

Library of Congress Cataloging-in-Publication Data applied for

ISBN 0 7190 5328 5 *hardback*
      0 7190 5329 3 *paperback*

First published 1999

06 05 04 03 02 01 00 99   10 9 8 7 6 5 4 3 2 1

Typeset in ITC Giovanni
by Carnegie Publishing, Lancaster
Printed in Great Britain
by Bell & Bain Ltd, Glasgow

Contents

Illustrations

Figures

Colour plates   *between pages* 34 *and* 35

Contributors

Janet Arnold

Editors' note: Sadly, Janet Arnold died shortly after completing her chapter in this volume. An earlier version of the following obituary was published in the *Daily Telegraph*, 26 November 1998.

Dress historian, born 6 October 1932, died of cancer on 2 November 1998

Janet Arnold was unique among dress historians brooking no interference in her tenacious pursuit and analysis of dress. Typically, in 1991 at the glittering private view of the exhibition to honour the couturier Hubert de Givenchy at the Palais Galliera, Paris, Janet was spotted, oblivious of the partying and the celebrities, hurrying from exhibit to exhibit, sketching as she went muttering, White Rabbit-like 'No time, no time'.

Janet was an artist who brought a scholarly discipline, an enthusiasm and, most significantly, a dressmaker's skill and practical understanding of the cut and construction of clothes to her life's work. This was to document surviving examples of historical dress by accurate line drawings, patterns and detailed descriptions – an endeavour that invigorated academic dress studies and provided a completely reliable source for costume designers. However, her route to pre-eminence was arduous and financially precarious.

In the immediate postwar years Janet was educated at Red Maids School and the West England College of Art, Bristol, obtaining a National Diploma of Design in Dress followed by teaching qualifications. In the mid-1950s she relished industrial and couture experience with the fashion houses, Frederick Starke and Victor Stiebel, and spent spare time helping in the wardrobe at London's Mermaid Theatre. A natural and inspirational communicator, her formal career in education began in 1955 as a lecturer at Hammersmith College, then from 1962–70 at Avery Hill College. Throughout this period she travelled extensively to visit theatres and study costume collections over Europe and the United States – which was at times difficult because Janet did not believe in travelling by aeroplanes.

Her initial researches were published in 1964 and 1965 in the first volumes of the innovative *Patterns of Fashion* series for Macmillan which were manna to students, costume and fashion designers as well as historians. Understanding the compelling power of fashion, in 1969 she originated the idea of exhibiting the costumes from the BBC's *The Six Wives of Henry VIII* at the V. & A. – one of the Museum's most popular exhibitions. In 1970, she was instrumental in organising the Museum of London's exhibition of costumes from the Corporation's *Elizabeth R* series.

From 1971 to 1975, she had a part-time fellowship at West Surrey College of Art after which she became a freelance lecturer. The 1970s were packed tight with commitments – writing the invaluable *A Handbook of Costume* (1973) researching costume and textiles from 1560 to 1620; teaching; compiling TV programmes and delving into collections and archives world-wide. By 1975, Janet had also started to write her major opus, *Queen Elizabeth's Wardrobe Unlock'd* (published in 1988). To her great pleasure, acknowledgement of her achievements arrived in the conferment of a Research Fellowship at the Royal Holloway College (1978) and she was elected a Fellow of the Royal Society of Antiquaries (1981).

Janet continued to be in constant demand, winning awards and scholarships to support her researches and museum consultancies though she always operated on a tiny budget. In 1983 she was invited to join the team in Florence at the Pitti Palace investigating and conserving the remarkable remains of the sixteenth-century Medici grave clothes worn by Eleonora of Toledo, Don Garzia de'Medici and Cosimo I – a project that lasted over ten years. Wherever sixteenth- and seventeenth-century clothes survived, from the Royal Armoury in Stockholm to the Germanisches National Museum, Nuremberg, Janet was on call for her expertise. Museums at home and abroad including the V. & A. felt possessive about Janet, as she was a delight to work with, having a wicked sense of humour and sharing her erudite discoveries gleefully. Her patterns of clothes for men and women 1560–1620 were published in 1985 with her crystal-clear line drawings and informed commentaries enabling costumiers to construct faithful replicas. Leading actresses including the late Peggy Ashcroft, Dame Judi Dench and Glenda Jackson have all worn costumes based on Janet's revelations and discovered that their accuracy added further authority to their per-formances.

Given the enormously time-consuming nature of her painstaking investigations that resembled forensic science, she was astoundingly prolific, making her discoveries available in standard texts and countless learned articles and catalogues. The University of West England recognised this immense contribution to dress history when they elevated Janet to professorial ranks in 1992. Though clearly in poor health in the 1990s, she refused to revise her punishing schedule, completing a lecture tour in America; returning to the collections in Stockholm and Florence; spending time in Prague with the grave clothes of Ferdinand I and at the Bayerisches Nationalmuseum Munich to review a collection of eighteenth-century garments. She was excited to be invited to partake in the publication of the *Mary Rose* finds and, in June 1998 was thrilled to receive the Globe Theatre's inaugural Sam Wanamaker Award. She has left two further volumes of *Patterns of Fashion* almost ready to go to press and fortunately, plans for a display of her work (which opened 1 February 1999) and a related study day (on 24 April) at the V. & A. were well in advance and honoured her achievements.

Valerie D. Mendes, Chief curator, textiles and dress, V. & A.

Juliet Ash is a senior lecturer in art and design history at Ravensbourne College of Design and Communication. She has co-edited with Lee Wright *Components of Dress* (Routledge, 1987) and with Elizabeth Wilson *Chic Thrills: A Fashion Reader* (HarperCollins, 1992 and 1996). She has also contributed articles on aspects of design history and theory to a number of publications.

Christopher Breward is reader in historical and cultural studies at London College of Fashion, The London Institute. He has published on several aspects of fashion and social identity and is currently working on the relationship between clothing and urban space in London between 1750 and 1990. Published work includes *The Culture of Fashion*

(Manchester University Press, 1995) and *The hidden consumer* (Manchester University Press, 1999).

Shaun Cole is assistant curator in the department of prints, drawings and paintings at the Victoria and Albert Museum. He worked as researcher for the Lesbian and Gay Styles and Skinhead sections of the Streetstyle exhibition held at the Victoria and Albert Museum, November 1994 to February 1995. He curated the Graphic Responses to Aids exhibition (1996) and co-curated Fashion on Paper (1997). He is currently researching a book on the history of gay men's dress.

Alicia Foster is an art historian whose particular areas of interest include women in modernism, urban spaces and identities and the interaction of high and popular culture. She was awarded a doctorate by Manchester University for her thesis on self-representation and constructions of femininity in the early work of Gwen John. She is currently preparing a book on Gwen John for the Tate Gallery's new series on British Artists.

Avril Hart has studied historical dress for over thirty years, working as a curator in the department of textiles and dress at the Victoria & Albert Museum. Her specialist areas have included extensive work into menswear, fans and eighteenth-century dress and she is actively involved in displaying the dress gallery, which opened in 1984. She has lectured and published, including three publications in 1998 for the Victoria & Albert Museum on *Ties, Historical Fashion in Detail* and *Fans*.

Amy de la Haye is a senior research fellow at the London College of Fashion, the London Institute and creative consultant to fashion designer Shirin Guild. Between 1992–98 she was curator of twentieth-century dress at the Victoria & Albert Museum, where she curated the Streetstyle (1993) and Cutting Edge (1997) exhibitions. She has published work on designer-level fashion, mass-produced dress and subculture style. Forthcoming work (with Valerie Mendes) includes *A Concise History of Twentieth-Century Fashion* (Thames & Hudson, World of Art series).

Aileen Ribeiro is head of the history of dress section at the Courtauld Institute and Reader in the history of art at the University of London. She has published many essays, articles and books on the history of dress and acted as a costume consultant to a number of exhibitions on painting. She specialises in the analysis of clothing in all forms of artistic media, and the ways in which artists represent reality and fantasy in dress. Among her recent publications are *The Art of Dress: Fashion in England and France 1750 to 1829* (Yale University Press, New Haven, 1999) and *Ingres in Fashion: Representations in Dress and Appearance in Ingres' Images of Women* (Yale University Press, New Haven, 1999). She is currently working on a book for the National Portrait Gallery on costume in portraiture.

Lou Taylor is professor of dress and textiles history at the University of Brighton, where she teaches undergraduate studies of fashion, decorative arts and design history as well as postgraduate researchers. She was presenter (and co-book author with Elizabeth Wilson) of the BBC's dress history series *Through the Looking Glass – A History of Dress From 1860 to the Present Day*. She has lectured widely and written extensively for books and journals, with other published work including her book *Mourning Dress* (Allen & Unwin, 1983) and a chapter on romantic couture evening and wedding dress for *The Cutting Edge: 50 Years of British Fashion* (Victoria & Albert Museum Publications, 1997).

Carol Tulloch is a part-time lecturer in visual culture at Middlesex University and the Royal College of Art. She has contributed to the publications *Chic Thrills: A Fashion Reader*

(HarperCollins, 1992 and 1996), *One-Off* (V. & A./RCA Design History Course) and the journal *Things*, as well as articles for the fashion press. Her exhibition works include Fashion on Paper: 1947–1997; Alphabet of a Century: Style, Taste and Society in Eighteenth Century London, an original idea by her and Alice Beard; Streetstyle: From Sidewalk to Catwalk and Rhapsodies in Black: Art of the Harlem Renaissance. Carol is currently working on a book based on dress and black culture.

Cordelia Warr completed her Ph.D. on 'Female Patronage and Female Spirituality in Italian Art of the Thirteenth and Fourteenth Centuries' in 1994 and is currently lecturer in art history at the University of Belfast. She spent two years living in Rome where she conducted research on the representation of religious dress in Italy in the later Middle Ages with funding from a Leverhulme Foundation postdoctoral scholarship. Dr Warr has published on the Baptistery in Padua (*Renaissance Studies*, 1996) and 'The Striped Mantle of the Poor Clares' (*Arte Cristiana*, 1998). Forthcoming articles include 'The Dominican Habit and the Vision of the Blessed Reginald of Orléans'.

Elizabeth Wilson is a professor of cultural studies at the University of North London. Among her publications are *Adorned in Dreams: Fashion and Modernity* (University of California Press, 1985), and *The Sphinx in the City* (University of California Press, 1993). With Juliet Ash she co-edited *Chic Thrills: A Fashion Reader* (Pandora, 1992). Her latest book, *Bohemians: From Scandal to Celebrity* will be published by I. B. Tauris in 2000.

1 ✧ Introduction

Elizabeth Wilson and Amy de la Haye

THE chapters in this volume originate from the 1995 Association of Art Historians' Conference. This was the first time that the Conference had a stream devoted to dress; it proved an opportunity to assess the advances made in this rapidly developing field and the convergence of perspectives from art and design history, sociology and anthropology, all of which have much to contribute to the study of a subject that is simultaneously economic, aesthetic, social and psychological. The papers were given by scholars from a wide range of disciplines, and the 'Dress Stream' was particularly inspiring and significant in bringing together pioneers in this once neglected field of research, in particular Janet Arnold, Avril Hart, Aileen Ribeiro, Valerie Mendes and Lou Taylor, alongside a new generation of young researchers, both groups having, of course, contributed so greatly to the growing importance and popularity of dress studies and its wider recognition.

The terms 'dress' and – even more so – 'fashion' have many different meanings, and the contemporary study of dress testifies to this diversity and to the importance of what we wear at every level of society. The manufacture and sale of clothing is a huge industry, both in Britain (where it is the fifth largest) and worldwide; it is therefore of major economic importance. At the same time dress performs a wide variety of important social functions. In the 1930s the psychoanalyst J. C. Flügel[1] saw it as a means of preserving our modesty while simultaneously exhibiting ourselves as sexual beings, and the erotic potential of dress (or the denial or concealment of the erotic) is certainly of great importance, but its social functions go far beyond this in signalling status, class and group affiliation, as Quentin Bell recognised in his classic study.[2] With the development of mass production, fashionable clothing has become central to mass culture in the widest sense as a means whereby individuals express themselves and construct identities. Finally, dress carries moral and political meanings. In the sixteenth and seventeenth centuries, governments in many European countries passed sumptuary laws intended to prevent the middling and lower orders from competing with the ruling class in the sumptuousness and extravagance of their garments, and rich dress was condemned by Christian moralists as evidence of sinfulness, worldliness and vanity. Such attacks were often simultaneously attacks on women.

In the late twentieth century, there are certain Islamic groups who advocate, or require women to wear forms of dress that hide their bodies, in order not to distract men. Two Malaysian beauty queens, for example, were arrested in August 1997 for having flouted these rules and displayed themselves in public dressed only in bathing costumes. Traditionally, western feminists have often been equally opposed to the excesses of fashionable dress, on grounds that were both similar and different. They, like religious fundamentalists, argued that fashion over-eroticised women and that it also, by using sweat-shop labour, exploited women as workers. Additionally, they condemned fashions designed by men for women – from the hooped and corseted fashions of the nineteenth century to Christian Dior's lavish and restrictive 1947 New Look, which was considered anachronistic, and, in the words of one woman Labour MP in Britain, as promoting the 'caged bird attitude'.[3] Where their arguments historically differed, and still differ from those advanced by religious fundamentalists, is that they never positioned women as temptresses; rather, they argue that it is men's responsibility to control their own impulses rather than requiring women to protect men, and that fashion, whether restrictive or over-eroticised, makes victims and 'sex objects' of women rather than predators. The most recent form this line of argument has taken is the suggestion that the excessively thin bodies of 'super waif' fashion models is to blame for the alleged increase in anorexia among adolescent girls, and the related idea that hard-core drugs are glamorised by the promotion of what has become known as 'heroin chic'.

Clearly, it is difficult to divorce analyses of fashion/dress from discussion of the human body. Dress, after all, and other kinds of body adornment, as Kaja Silverman wrote, 'make the human body culturally visible'.[4] As Eugenie Lemoine-Luccioni suggests, clothing draws the body so that it can be culturally seen, and articulates it as a meaningful form.[5] The Australian sociologist Jennifer Craik made a similar point in suggesting that 'we can regard the ways in which we clothe the body as an active process or technical means for constructing and presenting a bodily self', and she quoted the poem 'The Simultaneous Dress' by Blaise Cendrars, written for the designer Sonia Delaunay, which begins with the line 'On her dress she wears a body'.[6] Ultimately, the fact that we all wear clothes ensures the widespread appeal of the subject and makes everyone confident to express an opinion. However, this intimate and shared experience may perhaps also have contributed to the sometimes marginalised position that dress is given within academia and museology.

It is therefore not surprising that in recent years the sociological study of dress has shifted to incorporate the study of the human body, itself a growing area of study. The body is now explicitly understood not as a biological given but as a social construct producing multiple meanings. Dress is clearly part of that construction of meaning. On the other hand, the more traditional methodology of dress (often called costume) history was to examine the material culture as an independent entity: to focus, sometimes exclusively, upon object-based analyses. However, within museology and gradually within academia, historical and contemporary garments are increasingly being used as primary evidence for broader based contextual studies. A related field of enquiry is the study of dress as represented in paintings and especially portraiture, an area in which the work of Aileen Ribeiro has been particularly important (see Chapter 9 in this volume). The rich diversity of approaches towards the subject thus covers a spectrum, or continuum, from one end, at which a garment can be interpreted as an expression of the designer's creativity and craft skills, to the other, at which its construction and sale are considered as vital strands within economic history.

A further aspect of recent fashion studies is the challenge to the view that it is only in western capitalist societies that 'dress' becomes 'fashion'. This view was implicit, or taken for granted, in most works on fashion that were influential until the 1980s, when Elizabeth Wilson, for example, more explicitly advanced a definition of fashion as involving a cycle of changing styles that originated in the Burgundian court in the fourteenth century.[6] This view had already been challenged by Stella Mary Newton, who suggested that dress historians had been mistaken to perceive the dress of the European peasantry as unchanging and that even in the imperial courts of China and Japan there must have been 'fashions' in colours, ornamentation and other details, even if the shape of garments remained unchanging.[7] More recently, Joanne Eicher has challenged the idea that non-western dress is unchanging.

Historically, the dress of other cultures was usually studied by anthropologists, who had their own sets of concerns. Anthropology was interested in the collective social meanings of dress, but the clothes and ornamentation of non-western cultures was usually not understood as having a relationship of any kind to western dress. In the 1970s, however, sociologists studying British youth subcultures brought a similar perspective to bear on the 'uniforms' adopted by teddy boys, mods, rockers, skinheads and punks. Some of this work, which issued primarily from the pioneering studies undertaken at the Birmingham Centre for Contemporary Cultural Studies was gathered together in *Resistance Through Rituals*, edited by Stuart Hall and Tony Jefferson and published in 1976. The forms of resistance displayed by teds, mods and rockers was allegedly based on class antagonisms; in 1979 a seminal study of punk by Dick Hebdige foregrounded race rather than class. He interpreted the sometimes bizarre dress worn by these often alienated groups of youths in semiotic and cultural terms, elucidating the meaning of garments and adornment and the statements, simultaneously personal, aesthetic and political, made by these forms of dress.[8]

More recently, a number of writers have questioned the very possibility of 'subcultures of resistance' such as Hebdige and other cultural critics in the late 1970s judged as politically progressive. Ted Polhemus, for example, has suggested that young people today inhabit a 'supermarket of style' which is plundered at random and has little meaning other than in consumerist terms.[9] Sarah Thornton, too, sees subculture as assimilated to niche marketing and the commoditisation of 'cool', the politics of differences becoming a search for discrimination and distinction rather than opposition to the ruling order.[10] Michel Maffesoli has gone so far as to suggest that social cohesion has broken down and that contemporary society is wholly fragmented, leading to the abolition of the possibility of 'dominant' culture versus 'resistant' subculture as defined by Hebdige and his colleagues at the Birmingham Centre.[11] Hebdige and others were criticised, for example by Angela McRobbie,[12] for their concentration on masculine subcultures. The implication was that while young men were innovative in their use of dress to express dissidence and rebellion, young women were locked into a conventional and conservative enslavement to 'mainstream' fashion.

In terms of fashionable dress, this role was generally reversed and it is only quite recently that scholars such as Chris Breward, Shaun Cole, Richard Martin and Farid Chenoune have rescued men from what Flügel termed 'the great masculine renunciation'.[13] The new history and sociology of masculine dress are well represented in the current volume. It is now widely realised that the idea of the great masculine renunciation – the suggestion that with the coming of the industrial revolution men gave up all forms of ostentatious dress in favour of a dark, unchanging uniform – was, at best, greatly overstated. Nor were Flügel and Laver accurate in their explanation of fashion as an exclusively female phenomenon caused by women's narcissism, albeit in psychoanalytic rather than in purely pejorative terms. We are now more aware of the erotic aspect of men's dress: indeed much masculine dress produces an erotic masculinity precisely by means of disavowal. The changed perception of masculinity as a socially produced entity as artificial as femininity, is partly due to gay subcultures which emerged out of the closet and into the media, where gay constructions of masculinity have influenced advertising and magazine illustration, as well as spawning a number of gay life-style and lesbian magazines which actively embraced fashion in the 1990s. With these developments comes an increasing awareness that a number of popular music and club styles developed first in gay venues.

Debates about subcultural dress and style are concerned primarily with the social meaning of dress, although the V. & A.'s 1994 'Streetstyle' exhibition did focus upon the most visible aspect of subcultural identity – the clothes. Subcultures create collective meanings of the forms of dress they make their own, and thus their styles constitute statements to the world outside as well as signifying allegiance with group members. In the case of youth subcultures these meanings, as we shall see, have historically been interpreted as concerning rebellion and generational class and racial conflict. Within lesbian and gay subcultures the role of dress is different to the extent that, particularly in the past, dress codes could be a covert way of signalling the wearer's sexual preferences to other lesbians or gay men but without attracting unwelcome attention from the non-gay population at a period when homoeroticism was more taboo than it is today. As a result, these dress codes have become to some extent more simply celebratory, and certainly part of 'gay culture' as a subculture concerned with recognition and acceptance rather than rebellion and defiance, although they do, of course, still signal the sexual preferences of an individual.

Today there is less interest in the individual or even social psychology of clothes than earlier this century, when the psychological meanings of dress preoccupied predominantly male theoreticians seemingly, partly at least, because the 'vagaries of fashion' were associated with women, and perceived as irrational and in a sense meaningless. Using ideas deriving originally from dress reform movements, the influential writers of the first half of the twentieth century, such as Flügel, were concerned to explain how individuals ever came to consent to the wearing of fashions that were dismissed as 'ugly' or at best 'irrational'. At the end of the twentieth century we have moved away from this rather moralistic approach, although Alison Lurie, in the *Language of Clothes*, first published in 1981, revived it, seeing clothing as a language which punks, for example, could use as a means of expressing their infantile anger and suppressed longing to be mothered.[14] Fred Davis has pointed out that while clothes do 'make a statement', they cannot be grammatically parsed like a language in the way Alison Lurie attempts, and sees dress as communicating in a manner closer to music: an 'undercoded' form of communication expressive of mood and personality, certainly, but in a manner distinct from linguistic forms.[15]

Although what Roland Barthes termed 'the Fashion System' is a sign system, dress also functions as a vital part of the economy, and in recent years consumption studies have given dress due recognition, explicitly using it as one of the most reliable indexes charting the growth of consumer society.[16] The problem here can be that any sense of dress as fashion is lost in the study of dress as part of economic history. Nevertheless, in studying the history of dress from the perspective of our own epoch, in which some mass-produced clothes have become almost throwaway items, it is important to remember how valuable garments once were, items to be handed down from masters to servants, or, via a will, from one generation to the next, or used as items of exchange and barter.

Today, second-hand clothing is not just the preserve of the unemployed and those on social welfare, but also a fashionable and ecologically sound form of recycling clothes to achieve a unique personal style on a shoestring. This is especially true in Britain where artistic or bohemian and eccentric dress have long been worn by art students and in literary and artistic circles, as well as among aristocratic men and women, who combine antique, original ethnic and top-level fashion and bespoke garments. This demand is served by the plethora of specialist period clothing, second-hand and charity shops, as well as the auction houses and is reflected in the top-level fashion press, notably *Vogue* magazine and in new mass-market magazines such as *Cheap Chic*. Clearly, the wearing of old cashmere sweaters, tweeds and ball gowns which have been handed down from grandparents and parents is not so much about thrift as signifying family wealth and 'background'.

In the last twenty years the creation of *haute couture* has become a loss-making system of advertisement for highly profitable franchise lines such as scent and stockings, or as a form of what sometimes almost amounts to theatrical costume for a very few public figures. Nonetheless *haute couture* is still important as a laboratory of ideas and exploitation of the finest materials and craft skills. However, this is becoming less so as the market for couture has fallen to some two or three thousand clients worldwide, partly as a result of the recession and the anti-designer/conspicuous consumption backlash from the 1980s. Once ready-to-wear was the poor relation to *haute couture*, but increasingly it is the ready-to-wear collections which are being used to market licensed goods and lucrative diffusion lines. In spite of the rise of subcultural choices and the plurality of modern fashion, which reflects a fragmented, less homogeneous society, the designer as innovator continues to cut a significant figure. Fashion designers continue to exert a powerful influence upon the way we dress. The latest hemline might not make front-page news, but the international collections – made ever more popular by the supermodel phenomenon of the 1990s – continue to exert a major role within the media.

The success of the 1997 exhibition 'The Cutting Edge: Fifty Years of British Fashion' at the Victoria and Albert Museum in London, which attracted almost a quarter of a million visitors, demonstrated the enormous and wide-ranging public interest that exists in exclusive fashion, and there is room for more research into the role played by museum curators in extending public interest in, knowledge about and interpretation of fashionable dress. In the search for the representational meanings of dress, it is important that we do not lose sight of the role that dress historians and curators have always given to the garment as an object, to be investigated and displayed – depending upon the museum's emphasis – as an expression of design, social or technological circumstances. The selection and acquisition of historical and contemporary dress, as well as the ways in which it is displayed and interpreted, clearly influence our understanding of the past and modern day life as well as preparing us for the future.

Clothes, all in all, are enormously meaningful and are deeply entwined with our lives. In 1993 the Biba exhibition [17] (shown in Newcastle-upon-Tyne and Leicester, but not in London) recreated the ambience of the Biba shops in Kensington in the 1960s and early 1970s. It drew large crowds. A visitors' book solicited comments and the response was insightful – long entries amounting in some cases to autobiographical extracts as writers recorded in detail where, when and why they wore their first Biba garment and what it had meant to them – showing a whole generation of women whose identities had been formed by a culture in which the dresses of a particular designer had played a crucial role in establishing the ambience of the times. These women, now in their forties and fifties, were to be seen at the exhibition reminiscing with friends and reliving their youth.

In all its ramifications it is clear that 'fashion' can no longer be dismissed as trivial, unworthy and even – as used to be the case – immoral. Today, fashion in its various guises is widely accessible and relevant to so many aspects of life, yet in many respects it stands alone. For example, it simultaneously engages with the worlds of art, craft and industrial design and yet it belongs to none of them. It is both popular and élite and encompasses different forms of academic study with different purposes – the study of working-class and subcultural styles comes from a different tradition than that represented by the study of high fashion. The former sprang originally from ethnographic concerns and an interest in working-class life and youth groups, the latter came from design and art history and was driven initially by aesthetic concerns.

The scholarly work of the past two decades has brought about what almost amounts to a revolution in the way we conceptualise dress, and if, on the one hand, some may see this as being due to the dubious hedonism of a fully consumerised society, it is more fruitful to understand it as a recognition of the importance of daily life and also of 'history from below'. This book seeks to present a sample of the rich diversity and validity of the various approaches and areas of enquiry now being explored by those engaged in the study of dress today, as a demonstration of the historical, sociological and cultural importance of the clothes we wear.

Notes

1 J. C. Flügel, *The Psychology of Clothes*, London, Hogarth Press, 1930.

2 Quentin Bell, *Of Human Finery*, London, Hogarth Press, 1947. Bell is however over-reliant on and insufficiently critical of the theories of Thorstein Veblen, which exercised an undue influence on fashion researchers until recently, and an unfortunate one, given that Veblen was so hostile to fashion.

3 See Pearson Phillips, 'The New Look', in Michael Sissons and Philip French (eds), *The Age of Austerity 1945–1951*, Harmondsworth, Penguin, 1963; and Elizabeth Wilson, *Adorned in Dreams: Fashion and Modernity*, California, University of California Press, 1985.

4 Kaja Silverman, 'Fragments of a Fashionable Discourse', in Tanio Modleski (ed.), *Studies in Entertainment: Critical Approaches to Mass Culture*, Bloomington, Indiana, Indiana University Press, 1986, p. 147.

5 *Ibid.*, quoting Eugénie Lemoine-Luccioni, *La Robe*, Paris: Seuil, 1983.

6 Wilson, *Adorned in Dreams*, p. 3. See also Chandra Mukerji, *From Graven Images: Patterns of Modern Materialism*, New York, Columbia University Press, 1983.

7 Stella Mary Newton, 'Couture and Society', *Times Literary Supplement*, 12 November 1976.

8 Dick Hebdige, *Subculture: The Meaning of Style*, London, Methuen, 1979.

9 See Ted Polhemus, *Streetstyle: From Sidewalk to Catwalk*, London, Thames & Hudson, 1995.

10 See Sarah Thornton 'The Social Logic of Subcultural Capital', in Ken Gelder and Sarah Thornton (eds), *The Subcultures Reader*, London, Routledge, 1997, pp. 200–9; and Sarah Thornton, *Club Cultures: Music, Media and Subcultural Capital*, Cambridge, Polity Press, 1995. See also Caroline Evans, 'Dreams that Only Money Can Buy ... Or, The Shy Tribe in Flight from Discourse', in *Fashion Theory*, 1, (2) 1997, 169–88 for a comprehensive summary of these arguments.

11 Michel Maffesoli, *The Time of the Tribes: The Decline of Individualism in Mass Society*, London, Thousand Oaks, New Delhi, 1996.

12 Angela McRobbie and J. Garber, 'Girls and Subcultures', in S. Hall and T. Jefferson (eds), *Resistance Through Rituals*, London, Hutchinson, 1976; and Angela McRobbie, 'Working-Class Girls and the Culture of Femininity', in Women's Studies Group CCCS, editors, *Women Take Issue*, London, Hutchinson, 1978.

13 Flügel, *Psychology of Clothes*.

14 Alison Lurie, *The Language of Clothes*, London, Heinemann, 1981.

15 Fred Davis, *Fashion and the Construction of Identity*, Chicago, University of Chicago Press, 1993.

16 See for example Christopher Breward, *The Culture of Fashion*, Manchester, Manchester University Press, 1995, which is both a fashion history and a contribution to consumption theory.

17 See Tyne and Wear Museums, *Biba: The Label, The Lifestyle, The Look*, Newcastle-upon-Tyne, Tyne and Wear Museums, 1993. This, the catalogue of the exhibition, contains extracts from letters received during the 'Bring out your Biba' research campaign from 1991–92, containing memories of Biba garments and the shops.

2 ✧ Dashing Amazons: the development of women's riding dress, *c.* 1500–1900

Janet Arnold

O NE of the earliest references to a gown specifically for riding occurs in the privy purse expenses of Henry VII's consort, Elizabeth of York.[1] On 26 November 1502 thirteen yards of black satin were delivered to Robert Johnson, the Queen's tailor, for 'a riding gowne for the Quene at ixs the yerde'. A yard and a quarter of black velvet was used 'for an edge and cuffes for the same gowne at ixs vjd the yerde'. The gown was lined with seven yards of black buckram at ten pence per yard, with a nail [2¼ inches] of sarsenet 'for fentes [vents] for the same gown iiijd and for an elle quarter of canvas for lynyng of the same gown vjd'.

Tapestries and illuminated manuscripts show women on horseback at this period, but it is not clear if there was a particular style for riding dress. The ladies depicted in the illumination for the month of May in the *Très Riches Heures du Duc de Berri* manuscript[2] appear to be wearing impractical, highly fashionable clothes on horseback, riding side-saddle, in the early fifteenth century. Another lady, again in fashionable dress, in the month of August illumination, sits sideways behind a gentleman. There may be women's riding garments in the inventory of Henry VIII's property prepared in 1547, but the clerks did not describe them as such. However, 'a handle of a ryding rodd'[3] and 'one bagge of blewe bokeram with Riding roddes for gentilwomen' are listed:[4] Abraham de Bruyn's engraving of a Belgian noblewoman riding, which dates from 1576, shows one in use.[5] The Belgian lady wears a loosely cut garment with sleeves, which may be a 'jupe or gaskyn coat,' and a skirt, or petticoat, covering her feet, for riding, with a rather masculine-style hat (figure 1). Van Meteren wrote in 1575 that the English 'when they go abroad riding or travelling ... don their best clothes, contrary to the practice of other nations'.[6] Perhaps this fashion was set by Queen Elizabeth on her Progresses, but in 1563 Walter Fyshe, her tailor, made a 'round ryding kirtle of blac pynked velvet with bodies to the same, with a gard and ij weltes of blac velvet, lyned with blac Taffeta'.[7] A riding gown of 'blak velvet striped with silver and garded with crymsen velvet'[8] was altered in 1568, and had a new crimson taffeta

1 A Belgian noblewoman riding, holding a riding rod. Engraving from Abraham de Bryn, *Diversum Gentium Armatura Equestris*, 1576

lining put in. This was replaced in the following year: the riding gown probably had heavy wear.

Perhaps in the days when the horse was the principal form of transport a slight scent of horse sweat and a few hairs were acceptable on fashionable clothes, but for a long journey, or for hunting, riding garments were worn. Queen Elizabeth also had a riding cloak of wrought velvet lined with fur in 1563.[9] These items are the only ones, apart from hoods, to be listed as 'riding' clothes. Subsequently the Queen wore safeguards with doublets, jupes and cloaks, for riding.[10] Many of these cloaks are described as 'Dutch Cloaks' in the inventory of the Queen's Wardrobe of Robes, and would therefore have had sleeves, much easier for riding than a cloak. Turbervile shows the Queen out hunting, in the woodcuts in his books of 1575,[11] wearing fashionable dress with a masculine-style hat. The skirt does not seem to be 'a safeguard' or 'a kind of array or attire reaching from the navel to the feet', as it was described in 1585.[12] Moll Cutpurse, the outspoken, fearless leading character in the play *The Roaring Girl* by Middleton and Dekker, wears riding clothes and masculine breeches as an expression of her freedom and toughness. In one scene, the tailor discusses a new pair of breeches with her, described as 'great Dutch slops'.[13] She makes her first entrance in 'a freize jerkin and black saveguard',[14] so presumably the safeguard was a complete skirt rather than an apron front.

It seems to have been worn over breeches in Moll's case. Randle Holme described the safeguard as part of the 'Riding suite for women' in 1688.[15] It was 'put about the middle and so doth secure the feet from cold and dirt'. One green velvet safeguard worn by Queen Elizabeth, trimmed with carnation satin guards and gold and silver lace, had 'pockets and strings to it'.[16] The strings may have been tied round the foot or stirrup, to hold the skirt in position when mounted. This was a dangerous practice, which was certainly followed in the 1880s, with a tab and elastic stirrup.[17] A safety foot strap was invented in 1886.[18]

From the late 1580s onwards *juppes* seem to replace cloaks in Queen Elizabeth's wardrobe to a great extent. The term *juppe*, a name imported from France, was used in England in the late sixteenth century for a woman's upper garment usually accompanying a safeguard, apparently taking the place of a Dutch cloak. There are 43 *juppes* with matching safeguards listed for the Queen in the inventory of 1600.[19] They are in a wide range of colours and materials, including gold camlet, cloth of silver, velvet, satin, taffeta, lawn, grosgrain and network variously embroidered and decorated with gold and silver braids. The French origin of the *juppe* from *jupon*, is doubly confirmed with an entry in the New Year's Gift Roll of 1589, where 'a safeguard with a Jhup or gaskyn Coate of haire Cullored Satten',[20] trimmed with silver lace and buttons, was presented to the Queen by the Countess of Shrewsbury. Gascons were natives of Gascony, a province of south-western France. Many were soldiers of fortune and spent much time on horseback. The 'juppe or gaskyn coat' may therefore have copied some feature common to the riding coats worn by these men. It was probably a loose form of doublet, comfortable for riding, but fitting more closely than a Dutch cloak. *Juppe* may be an alternative name for a cassock, a garment which women had worn in the 1540s and 1550s, but this can only be conjecture. Queen Elizabeth wears a fashionably trained gown in illustrations of the hunt in Turbervile's books on hunting printed in 1575,[21] and there is, apparently, no visual evidence of *juppe* and safeguard, both garments listed in the inventory of the wardrobe of robes prepared in 1600.

It may have been the introduction of the masculine style of 'juppe or gaskyn coat' which gave the impetus for the adoption of other masculine fashions of doublet, jacket and jerkin. Philip Stubbes complained in 1583 that 'the women also there have dublettes and jerkins, as men have here, buttoned up the breast, and made with winges and weltes ... as mannes apparell is, for all the worlde and though this be a kind of attire appropriate only to man yet they blushe not to wear it'.[22] Queen Anne of Denmark is ready to ride in a deep-green gown accompanied by her dogs, the horse behind her, held by a black servant, in Paul van Somer's painting of

2   Elizabeth of Bohemia, riding astride, watercolour from Adriaen van de Venne's
Album, 1626

1617.[23] Her hat follows masculine lines and she wears severely practical
leather gloves: her sleeves, slashed at the tops, also follow the masculine
fashion. The low neckline is filled in with a partlet of white tucked linen.
There is no indication that the Queen wears anything other than the skirt
of a gown; it does not seem to be a safeguard.

Most paintings show women riding side-saddle, but there are a few
examples of what appear to be women riding astride, such as the Princess
of Orange in a riding party on the Bienenhof dating from around
1620.[24] A little water colour by Adrian van der Venne, dating from 1626,[25]
gives the clear impression that James I of England's daughter Elizabeth,
Queen of Bohemia, is riding astride in a gown of the palest pink silk with
a woven pattern, trimmed with gold lace and lined with blue silk (figure 2).
A small painting of the same subject, by the same artist, also dated 1626,[26]
shows her in the same pose, and it certainly seems to be astride. It is not
clear if breeches were worn beneath a skirt buttoning down the front, but
it seems very likely. Velázquez's portrait of Queen Isabella painted around
1630 [27] shows what may be a safeguard, with an immense amount of
material spread over the back of the horse.

Daniel Mytens' painting of King Charles I and Queen Henrietta Maria,
standing together before departing for the chase, also dates from around
1630.[28] The Queen's gown is fairly severe in line, with rows of lace (braid)

trimming and the masculine-style hat which is very much like that worn by her husband. Margaret Lemon wears a similar hat in her miniature by Samuel Cooper, his earliest-known signed work, painted around 1635.[29] She is often described as wearing masquerade dress, with a masculine-style doublet, Flemish bobbin lace collar, and felt hat. However, it is more likely that this is a riding habit following the masculine fashions, as Philip Stubbes commented: 'as mannes apparell is, for all the worlde'.[30]

There are very few examples of women's clothing remaining from the early seventeenth century, but among them is one doublet with high collar, shoulder wings and sleeves [31] which give the impression that it was worn by a slim young man, or a youth. However, although it may originally have been a youth's doublet of around 1625, the crease marks and stitching, and also the shape of the back when mounted on a stand,[32] reveal that shortly after this date the garment was certainly altered for a slim young woman, or a girl, to wear (figure 3). Further alterations were made for it to be worn again, by a slightly larger woman, as fancy dress, in the nineteenth century. The doublet is made of rich tan satin, now faded to a warm pinkish peach, and is decorated with bands of embroidery, arranged diagonally on the sleeves, front and back. The sleeves are cut in the Spanish style, the *manga redonda*, or 'round sleeve' as it was described in England. The back is curved to lie smoothly over a dome-shaped petticoat. An embroidered panel is let in at the side seam to enlarge the garment, a contemporary alteration.[33] At the centre front waist there are two pairs of eyelet holes on each side, as are seen on men's doublets. However, on the left front two buttonholes have been worked over them, in silk of a different shade,[34] and by a different hand from the tailor who worked the other buttonholes. All these buttonholes are pulled out of shape with use,

3 Woman's doublet or cassock in rich tan satin decorated with bands of embroidery

except the two worked over the eyelet holes, so the garment was probably worn a number of times before the alterations. This was the first piece of evidence that the doublet might have been worn first by a youth and then by a girl or young woman. Comparison with the insides of men's doublets of this period showed that the triangular belly-piece, and reinforced strip round the waist with metal rings, to attach to hooks on the waistband of the breeches, were not put in. The pattern of the doublet is almost identical to a pattern for a *calcon y ropilla* given in a Spanish tailor's pattern book by La Rocha Burguen, printed in 1618.[35] Minsheu translates this as 'breeches, or slops' and a 'cassock'.[36] The *ropilla*, or cassock was semi-fitting and intended for wear over a doublet, so it would not have had a belly-piece and waist-strip when it was first made. It would thus have been easily adapted to a woman's figure with the two strips let in at the side seams. The second wearer may have described this doublet as 'in the style of a cassock' or perhaps called it a cassock 'in the style of a doublet.' Early seventeenth-century terminology can be confusing, but Minsheu[37] gives the English translation of the Spanish *ropilla* as cassock and Cotgrave[38] gives the French term *juppe* for cassock. As we have already seen, Queen Elizabeth wore *juppes* with safeguards for riding. This is an early and most interesting example of riding dress (figure 3).

Queen Christina of Sweden was a notable horsewoman. An engraving records her triumphal entry into Rome on 23 December 1655,[39] when she rode on a beautiful palfrey superbly saddled and housed in blue and silver, the Pope's gift. She wore a simple grey gown, a black scarf and plumed hat. Her only jewellery was a gold ring. She must have been the focus of all eyes, a plain figure in the centre of an overwhelming display of splendour, riding side-saddle. She also rode side-saddle on her entry into Paris in 1656, on a grey horse named Unicorn, loaned for the occasion by the Duc de Guise. This entry was also recorded in an engraving, which shows her wearing a loosely fitting upper garment, possibly a cassock.[40] When she arrived at Compeigne the next day Madame de Mottville noted in her diary[41] that Christina's wig was uncurled and her hair blowing over her face. Her clothes were extraordinary, more like a man's than a woman's, with skirts so short that her feet showed: however, the Queen's personality triumphed over her clothes. In the portrait by Sebastian Bourdon[42] Christina wears what is almost certainly a cassock, with a man's cravat[43] tied with a black ribbon at the neck, riding side-saddle.

One of the earliest French tailors' books, Benoit Boullay's *Le Tailleur Sincère*, printed in 1671, gives a pattern diagram of a garment similar to that worn by Queen Christina.[44] It is described as a '*manteau de femme à cheval,*' and is cut with a half circle to give fullness at the back. The sleeve is pleated where necessary to fit the armhole and 'The front is adjusted to fit the body by means of two wide ribbons, which are attached under the fronts at points beside the armholes. The ribbons wind round the back, so that the material in the back and sides is pleated and floats gracefully'. There is no mention here yet of the term *en tenue Amazone* which was used for riding dress in France.

The term 'riding habit' seems to be first mentioned by John Evelyn in his diary on 13 September 1666 when 'The Queen was now in her cavalier riding habit'. In 1711, Steele wrote of the 'Amazonian Hunting Habit' in an amusing description of an encounter by John Hughes with

> a little party of horsemen ... my whole attention was fixed on a very fair youth who rode in the midst of them, and seemed to have been dressed by some description in a romance. His features, complexion and habit had a remarkable effeminacy, and a certain languishing vanity appeared in his air. His hair, well curled and powdered, hung to a considerable length on his shoulders, and was wantonly tied, as if by the hands of his mistress, in a scarlet ribband, which played like a streamer behind him; he had a coat and waistcoat of blue camlet trimmed and embroidered with silver; a cravat of the finest lace; and wore in a smart cock, a little beaver hat edged with silver, and made more sprightly by a feather ... I perceived on my nearer approach, and as I turned my eyes downward, a part of the equipage I had not observed before, which was a petticoat of the same with the coat and waistcoat. After this discovery, I looked again on the face of the fair Amazon who had thus deceived me, and thought these features which before had offended me by their softness, were now strengthened into an improper boldness ... The model of this Amazonian hunting-habit for ladies, was, I take it, first imported from France, and well enough expresses the gaiety of a people who are taught to do anything, so be it with an assurance; but I cannot help thinking it fits awkwardly yet on English modesty. The petticoat is an encumbrance upon it, and if the Amazons should think fit to go on in this plunder of our sexes ornaments, they ought to add to their spoils, and complete their triumph over us, by wearing the breeches.[45]

The word 'habit' is used here in the sense of clothing or attire, and his use of the word 'Amazonian' suggests that the term *en tenue Amazone* was in use by the late seventeenth century in France.

In the late seventeenth century, fashionable women copied men's fashions very closely for riding dress, even to the wigs. Samuel Cooper's miniature of Frances Stewart, Duchess of Richmond and Lennox, a Maid of Honour to Catherine of Braganza, painted in 1666, shows her wearing a wig, plumed hat and cravat.[46] Pepys described this style in his diary on 12 June 1666:

> Walking in the Galleries at Whitehall, I find the Ladies of Honour dressed in their riding garbs with coats and doublets with deep skirts, just for all

the world like mine, and buttoned their doublets up the breast, with periwigs and with hats: so that, only for a long petticoat dragging under their men's coats, nobody could take them for women in any point whatever; which was an odd sight, and a sight that did not please me. It was Mrs Wells and another fine lady that I saw thus.

Although the miniature of Frances Stuart only shows hat, wig, cravat and top half of the coat, it is sufficiently like the description Pepys gives of the other two Maids of Honour to be fairly certain that it is a riding habit. Anthony Wood also described this fashion in 1665

women would strive to be like men, viz., when they rode on horseback or in coaches weare plush caps like monteros, either full of ribbons or feathers, long periwigs which men used to weare, and riding coate of a red colour all bedaubed with lace which they call vests, and this habit was chiefly used by the ladies and maids of honor belonging to the Queen, brought in fashion about anno 1663, which they we[a]re at this time [1665] of their being in Oxon.[47]

Several paintings attributed to Pierre Mignard show similar fashionable French riding habits in the early 1680s. Catherine de Nenfville-Villeroy, Contesse d'Armagnac,[48] wears a fashionable cravat with ornamental cravat strings of ribbon beneath, a masculine fashion. She seems to be wearing her own hair tightly curled or 'coiffé hurluberlu' as Madame de Sévigné described it in a letter dated 1 April 1671. A shoulder knot, a bunch of ribbon loops, is stitched to her right shoulder. This fashion is seen for men from around 1665 to the 1680s. Anne de Souvré de Courtanvaux, Marquise de Louvois,[49] wears a similar habit, with a hat of masculine style, trimmed with feathers. Her sash flies out and a pocket handkerchief with knotted corners is tucked into her pocket. Marie de la Motte-Houdancourt, Duchesse de la Ferté,[50] shows the opening at the centre back skirts of her coat, which is heavily trimmed with lace, or braid, after the masculine fashion (figure 4). Anne Marie Mancini, Duchesse de Bouillon,[51] has her hair tied back with two ribbon bows. Her coat swings back to reveal a waistcoat beneath. All these women wear practical leather gloves with cuffs trimmed either with fringe or loops of ribbon. Portraits of men on horseback, hats trimmed with feathers, and long wigs, show the source of inspiration for these fashionable habits. One French engraving dating from around 1690,[52] of a young woman in hunting dress holding a gun, shows a long cravat caught through a buttonhole in the masculine style, and called a Steinkerk. The fashion took its name from the battle fought in 1692, though it had been seen just before that date. The mask she carries in her hand would have protected her face from the elements.

Although all the petticoats worn by the French women in these portraits attributed to Mignard are in richly patterned silks, either woven or embroidered, woollen or worsted cloth was also used. Marie Adelaide of Savoy, Duchess of Burgundy, was painted by Pierre Gaubert around 1690 [53] wearing a scarlet cloth habit, a colour that would later be described as 'hunting pink' in England, from the early nineteenth century onwards. Eighteenth-century sporting paintings show women riding side-saddle in the habits of the various hunts, distinctive uniforms still following the masculine styles, and cut in hard-wearing cloth.

At the end of the seventeenth century, women gradually took over the work of making women's clothes from men, but tailors continued to make women's riding habits, and it continues to be a branch of tailoring to the

4 *Marie de la Motte-Houdancourt, Duchesse de la Ferté*, attributed to Pierre Mignard, *c.*1680–85

facing 5 Lady Evelyn Pierrepoint in a riding habit with full wig, tricorne hat, and cravat. Miniature by Bernard Lens, *c.*1711–12

present day. Lady Evelyn Pierrepoint, painted by Bernard Lens around 1711–12,[54] wears one of these fashionable habits, with braid froggings, across the front 'after the Polish fashion,'[55] fastening with big buttons (figure 5). Her wig is full and heavily curled. Sir Godfrey Kneller's portrait of Henrietta Cavendish, Lady Huntingtower, dates from about 1715.[56] Her short, full-bottomed wig is worn with a masculine-style hat and cravat. The wide buttoned cuffs and pocket flaps of the cream-coloured coat, with heavy gold lace (braid), again echo the masculine fashions. Another portrait by Kneller, of the Countess of Mar, painted in 1715,[57] shows the matching pale-pink cloth waistcoat beneath the coat, all heavily laced with silver. John Gay wrote in the *Guardian* in 1713: 'There is another kind of occasional dress in use among the Ladies, I mean the riding habit, which some have not injudiciously stiled the Hermaphroditical, by reason of its Masculine and Feminine composition.'[58] The habit was not only riding dress, but was used for travelling. When the Duchess of Queensberry was in Europe in 1734 she must have worn a habit, for her brother wrote that she had been called 'Sir' upon the road more than twenty times.[59] However, the habit, with its masculine cut, was also accepted in England as an alternative morning dress, for informal wear. It is, indeed, the forerunner of the woman's tailored suit.

The masculine styles for habits continued in the eighteenth century, the fashionable silhouette of women's fashions achieved by the stays and petticoats worn beneath. Lancret's painting of *The Picnic after the Hunt*,[60] dating from around 1740 shows a group of French women wearing hooped petticoats. A white silk waistcoat is obviously pushed out by the hoop under the scarlet cloth petticoat, and the bottom buttons have been left undone. The hoops would have collapsed to allow for mounting the horse, but might have presented a hazard if the rider was thrown on the hunting field. A small painting of a stag hunt by James Seymour[61] some ten years later shows two English women wearing uniform blue cloth habits, laced with gold. The leading rider, in a three-quarter view, shows the jacket buttoned at the front, fitting over an upright figure supported by the appropriate stays. At the right side there appears to be a strap fastened round her skirt and this feature may be seen more clearly in the side view of the second rider. This is presumably to hold the skirt in position when galloping, as it only just covers the feet. The jacket is lined with red silk and her neat black jockey cap matches those worn by all the huntsmen. Joanna von Schmerfeld wears a similar cap in her portrait by Tischbein painted around 1760.[62] It is trimmed with a grey feather and a knot of white ribbon. Her habit seems to be made of green velvet, or possibly a superfine cloth. It fastens with 'froggings' in curling gold leaf shapes with small gold tassels. The cuffs and front are bordered with gold lace. It is easy to understand why a habit as attractive as this was used for informal wear as well as for riding.

A number of eighteenth-century riding habits survive in museum collections. One jacket from the Snowshill collection, dating from around 1730–50,[63] is in deep drab-coloured worsted cloth and has cuffs and collar faced with matching velvet. It is lined in the skirts with rose-pink silk taffeta. The tailor has solved the awkward problem of fitting a woman's figure, supported by a pair of stays stiffened with whalebone, by putting a dart across the front. The shape of the skirts follow the lines of a man's coat to achieve the pleats at the side, with a waist seam to fit the figure closely above. Another jacket, with matching petticoat, in pink silk and worsted mixture dating from around 1775–80 is cut in a similar way, with turn-down collar.[64] The lapels are fastened back with silver buttons and the sleeves have cuffs *à la marinière*. The fronts fasten edge to edge with hooks and eyes. The style was inspired by the Hussars' uniform.[65] The matching petticoat is cut in straight widths pleated to fit the waist, and just clears the feet when walking. Another habit with the same features, and with a matching waistcoat, is made of crimson woollen broadcloth and dates from the 1770s.[66] This petticoat also clears the ground. This may be the reason for the strap passing round the skirt in James Seymour's painting of the stag hunt. The seventeenth-century petticoats dragged on the ground, and there was plenty of material to cover the feet when riding side-saddle.

Henry Styleman and his first wife Mary Gregg, were painted by Zoffany around 1780.[67] Her jacket is cut away from the front, following the new lines of men's coats. This development continues, the waist slowly rising, following women's fashions, while still retaining the tailored lines, though not with the entire approval of the tailors. As *The Taylor's Complete Guide* commented in 1796:

> The present mode of making Riding Habits is much out of the regular method, for such short waists and broad lapels, buttons set so wide, and other ingenious maxims that the maker, with all his application, is totally incapable of setting the beautiful finishing of nature in any point of view fit for public inspection … What will future workmen say when we declare the difference and quick transition of fashion in these particulars between 1793, when we were wont to cut waists full nine inches long from under the arm down to the hip … and in the year 1796 we have been obliged to cut them but three inches in the same place. [68]

A light-blue cloth riding habit in the Salisbury Museum collection,[69] dating from around 1795–1810, has a skirt so long that it would have to be held up, or carried over the arm, until mounted on horseback. There are tapes and tabs inside which, when tied up, enable the habit to be worn for walking.

By the time that Jane Austen wrote the words 'Her habit therefore was thrown off with all possible haste' in *Northanger Abbey* in 1798,[70] the word 'habit' had become synonymous with 'riding habit,' and was used for travelling and walking as well as riding. Catherine Morland travelled first in General Tilney's chaise and four, and then in Henry Tilney's curricle, from Bath to Northanger Abbey wearing a habit with a new straw bonnet. On arrival, 'having given a good shake to her habit' to remove the moisture from 'a thick mizzling rain ... she was ready to be shewn into the common drawing-room'.[71]

The Lady's Monthly Museum of September 1808 comments that 'Habits are very appropriate for travelling costume and are at this period constructed with more than usual grace'. The front of the jacket of this habit is cut on the cross, and fitted closely, with two darts and light padding over the bust. The padding makes a smooth line to the shoulder. A similar pattern diagram for a jacket is given in *The Taylor's Complete Guide*, with another, which is cut in one piece on the cross grain of the fabric.[72] The skirt of the Salisbury habit is made from a 137-cm (54 inches) wide straight panel at the front and a narrow, slightly gored one at the back. The back skirt is tightly gathered in to fit the waist and the front is left smooth. There is a small taffeta bodice to which the skirt is attached, and a little bustle pad of taffeta wadded with wool to hold out the skirt at the back, beneath the short skirts of the jacket.[73] A similar habit, with the long skirt hanging down far below the feet, may be seen in Henry Bernard Chalon's painting of the Warwickshire Beagles in 1813.[74] Again, the lady follows the gentlemen in the matter of headgear, with a hat with a tall crown. This skirt would have been tied, or hooked up, for walking. These habits, in firm woollen or worsted cloths, from the eighteenth century onwards (as arranged for walking) are the forerunners of women's tailored suits of the 1890s.

There are several editions of George Walker's *The Tailor's Masterpiece* and in the instructions and pattern layout for the riding habit in the 1838 edition he mentions styles of 1817, 1827, 1834 and 1837, and gives the variations in sleeve styles.[75] Drawings of the habit show first the skirt tied up for walking, and then trailing on the ground, ready to mount the horse.[76] Achille Deveria's watercolour *Sept heures du matin* shows a similar riding habit with a masculine-style hat worn with a veil, and masculine neckwear, around 1835.[77] The same fashion features are seen in a surviving bottle-green broadcloth habit.[78] A paper label stitched to the skirt reads: 'Mother's wedding dress made in 1831, Philadelphia. Norah V. Reynolds and Thomas Williams married in Wilmington, Delaware, May 5th 1831'.

6   Dark green and black riding habits worn with top hats and veils, *Corriere delle Dame*, 10 March 1842

At knee level, inside the skirt, is stitched a white tape with hooks sewn to it, and there are worked loops at the hemline, to hold the length up for walking. The skirt is cut in straight panels, without any gores, and is pleated in to fit the waist of the natural linen bodice. This opens at the back with hooks and eyes. Two riding habits of 1842 show the masculine-style hats worn with veils (figure 6).

By the 1850s there were habits with matching breeches, some partly of chamois leather, a number of which are preserved in Museum collections.[79] An increasing number of tailors' books explain increasingly complicated

Section IV. RIDING GARMENTS.

7 Riding garments, T. H. Holding, *Direct System of Ladies Cutting*, 1901
8 G. W. Clarke's safety habit skirt, T. H. Holding, *Direct System of Ladies Cutting*, 1901

cutting systems. Every tailor had his own way of cutting a riding skirt, particularly after the shaping for the knee appeared from the 1870s onwards. 'Holdings New Safety Train' is just one example of the tailor's ingenuity.[80] Instead of a pocket shape for the pommel of the side saddle, there is a hole, so that the habit fits better when mounted. Holding comments that the lady 'must have on breeches or knickerbockers'. These riding habit skirts are a very strange shape when dismounted. The rider had to catch the whole skirt round her legs in a drapery when walking across the yard. Another of these safety trains was described thus: 'Whilst being little more than an apron, this train can, if desired, be partly buttoned, so that it may be carried in such a manner as not to show trousers when the wearer is dismounted.'[81]

A selection of riding garments in 1901[82] shows how much they still owe to masculine fashions (figure 7). They are 'tailor-made' from firmly

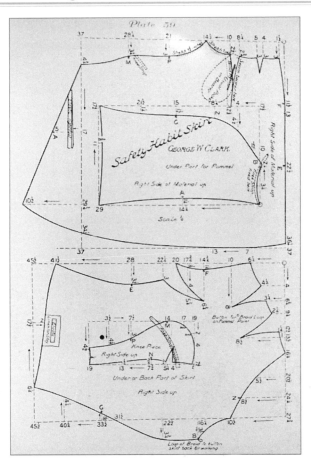

9 G. W. Clarke's safety
habit skirt pattern
diagram, T. H. Holding,
*Direct System of Ladies
Cutting,* 1901

woven, hard-wearing cloth, that will endure through rainstorms, being splashed with mud, and taken through briars and hedges, let alone contact with the saddle and the horse. A garment made by a dressmaker would not stand up to such hard wear. It is not surprising that habits followed masculine fashions, and were made by tailors.

Another safety habit skirt of 1901 has elastic straps for the heel, to prevent the skirt from riding up under the seat (figures 8 and 9).[83] The safety feature is a strap inside the habit to be fastened round the knee before mounting; 'The skirt is then absolutely safe, as the lady cannot possibly leave the saddle without bringing the habit with her'. These habit skirts required a great deal of careful fitting and the instructions for Clarke's safety habit skirt warned

Do not attempt to make a close-fitting Habit unless you can see it on a saddle. If you don't possess a proper trying-on block, you can adopt a plan

I tried successfully 15 years ago. I got four chairs and set them back to back, two in front and two behind, leaving sufficient space between to allow a large piece of Melton to lie on the top. These, I fixed securely together, and strapped a saddle on ... My customer smiled when she saw the mount, but the Habit was a success and that was all she cared about. If anyone should try this, be sure to test the structure before allowing the lady on the saddle.[84]

Notes

1 Nicholas Harris Nicolas, *Privy Purse Expenses of Elizabeth of York*, 1830, pp. 68–9.

2 The *Très Riches Heures du Duc de Berri* manuscript, executed by Pol de Limbourg and his brothers between 1409–16, in the collection of the Musée Condé, Chantilly, has been reproduced in many full colour facsimile editions.

3 BL, Harl. MS 1419A, f. 186v.

4 *Ibid.*, f. 509v, f. 118r, f. 469v.

5 Abraham de Bruyn, *Diversum Gentium Armatura Equestris*, 1576.

6 William Brenchley Rye, *England as Seen by Foreigners in the Days of Elizabeth and James the First*, 1865, p. 71.

7 PRO, LC5/33, f. 39, warrant dated 4 May 1563, cited in Janet Arnold, *Queen Elizabeth's Wardrobe Unlock'd*, Leeds, W. S. Manley, 1988, p. 141.

8 BL, Egerton 2806, f. 9, warrant dated 16 October 1568, cited in *ibid.*

9 PRO, LC5/33, f. 64, warrant dated 2 November 1563, cited in *ibid.*

10 Arnold, *Wardrobe*, pp. 141–2.

11 Illustrated in *ibid.*, Figures 226, 227.

12 John Higgins, *The Nomenclator, or Remembrancer of Adrianus, Junius, written in Latine, Greeke, French and other forrein tongues and now in English*, 1585.

13 Thomas Middleton and Thomas Dekker, *The Roaring Girl*, written *c.* 1608, published 1611, London, New Mermaid edition 1976, p. 49.

14 *Ibid.*, p. 33.

15 Randle Holme, *Academy of Armory, or a Storehouse of Armory and Blazon*, Chester, 1688, facsimile edition, Menston, 1972, III, p. 95.

16 BL, Egerton 2806, f. 86, cited in Arnold, *Wardrobe*, p. 142.

17 Irene Foster, 'The Development of Riding Costume *c.* 1880–1920' in *Costume*, 3, 1969, p. 56.

18 *Ibid.*

19 BL, Stowe 557, ff. 76–9/1–43, printed in Arnold, *Wardrobe*, pp. 313–16.

20 New Year's Gift Roll, 31 Eliz. 1589. BL, Lansd. Roll 17, cited in *ibid.*, pp. 142, 315.

21 George Turbervile, *The Noble Art of Venerie*, 1575 and *The Book of Falconrie*, 1575, illustrated in *ibid.*, Figures 226, 227.

22 Philip Stubbes, *The Anatomie of Abuses*, 1583 edition, p. 37.

23 Illustrated in colour in Graham Reynolds, *Elizabethan and Jacobean 1558–1625*, 1951, Plate 38. A contemporary replica is illustrated in Karen Hearn (ed.), *Dynasties:*

Painting in Tudor and Jacobean England 1530–1630, London, Tate Gallery, 1995, cat. no. 139.

24 H. A. Pacx, *The Princess of Orange on the Bienenhof, c. 1620*, the Mauritshuis, the Hague.

25 Illustrated in colour in Martin Royalton-Kisch, *Adriaen van de Venne's Album*, London, British Museum, 1988, p. 167.

26 Illustrated in *ibid.*, p. 15

27 Velázquez, *Queen Isabel of Bourbon, Consort of Philip IV of Spain*, 1631, illustrated in colour in Dale Brown, *The World of Velázquez 1599–1660*, New York, 1969, p. 75.

28 Daniel Mytens, *King Charles I and Queen Henrietta Maria departing for the Chase, c. 1630*, illustrated in Janet Arnold, 'An Early Seventeenth Century Woman's Riding Doublet or Cassock,' in *Waffen-und Kostümkunde*, 1980, Part 1, p. 124.

29 Illustrated in colour, Daphne Foskett, *Samuel Cooper and His Contemporaries*, London, National Portrait Gallery, exhibition catalogue, No. 9, where she is described as 'dressed as a young cavalier'.

30 Stubbes, *Anatomie*, p. 37.

31 This is discussed in detail, with pattern diagrams, in Arnold, 'Cassock,' pp. 113–28.

32 *Ibid.*, Figures 2 and 3.

33 *Ibid.*, Figures 2, 7 and 21.

34 *Ibid.*, Figures 10 and 11.

35 *Ibid.*, Figure 20.

36 John Minsheu, *The Guide into Tongues*, 1617.

37 John Minsheu, *A Dictionarie in Spanish and English*, 1599.

38 Randle Cotgrave, *A Dictionarie of the French and English Tongues*, 1632.

39 Illustrated in Georgina Masson, *Queen Christina*, 1968, 1974 edition, facing p. 320.

40 Pierre Mariette, *Queen Christina arriving in Paris*, 1656, engraving, Stockholm, Kungl. Biblioteket.

41 Masson, *Queen Christina*, p. 276.

42 The Prado, Madrid, illustrated in colour, *ibid.*, cover.

43 Thomas Blount, *Glossographia*, 1656, gives cravat as 'a new fashioned gorget which women wear,' presumably following the masculine fashion.

44 Pattern and instructions for cutting a lady's riding coat in Janet Arnold, *Patterns of Fashion: English Women's dresses and their construction c. 1660–1860*, London, 1964, new edition 1977, p. 3.

45 Richard Steele, the *Spectator*, Friday 29 June 1711, No. 104.

46 Illustrated in Foskett, *Samuel Cooper*, cat. No. 119.

47 *The Life and Times of Anthony Wood, Antiquary of Oxford, 1632–95, described by himself*, collected by Andrew Clark, Oxford, Oxford Historical Society, 1891, Vol. I, p. 509.

48 Skoklosters Slott, Inv. No. 3149. The cravat may be compared with Nicolas de Largillière, *Young Man and his Tutor*, 1685, in the National Gallery, Washington, DC, Inv. No. 1961.9.26.

49 Skoklosters Slott, Inv. No. 3145. Illustrated in Arnold, 'Cassock,' Figure 19.

50 Skoklosters Slott, Inv. No. 3148.

51 Skoklosters Slott, Inv. No. 3416.

52 Bibliothèque Nationale, illustrated in Gisele d'Assailly, *Ages of Elegance*, 1968, p. 104.

53 Versailles Museum, illustrated in colour, *ibid.*

54 *Lady Evelyn Pierrepoint*, married 1711/12 John, Earl Gower, miniature by Bernard Lens, in a private collection.

55 For an explanation of the Polish fashion, see Arnold, *Wardrobe*, pp. 136–8.

56 Ham House, Inv. No. H.H. 231–1948.

57 National Portrait Gallery of Scotland, illustrated in C. Willett Cunnington and P. Cunnington, *A Picture History of English Costume*, London, 1960, Figure 182.

58 The *Guardian*, No. 149, 1713.

59 Henrietta, Countess of Suffolk, *Letters*, 1824, II, p. 98, cited in Anne Buck, *Dress in Eighteenth Century England*, London, Batsford, 1979, p. 52.

60 National Gallery of Art, Washington, DC, Inv. No. Kress 1952-2-22.

61 *British Sporting Painting 1650–1850*, Hayward Gallery, London Arts Council catalogue, 1974, cat. No. 28, private collection.

62 Germanisches National Museum, Nürnberg, Inv. No. GM 1334.

63 Illustrated in Arnold, *Patterns*, pp. 24–5.

64 Hereford Museum, Inv. No. 4983, publication of drawings, pattern and details, forthcoming.

65 For example see the painting of Francis Vincent in green and red Hussar uniform, dated 1763, illustrated in *Polite Society by Arthur Devis 1712–1787*, London, National Portrait Gallery exhibition catalogue 1983, cat. No. 50.

66 Illustrated in *Four Hundred Years of Fashion*, London, Victoria and Albert Museum catalogue, 1984, cat. No. 15, acc. no. 269 to B–1890.

67 *British Sporting Painting*, cat. No. 63.

68 Cited in Arnold, *Patterns*, p. 8.

69 Illustrated, with pattern, *ibid.*, pp. 46–7.

70 Jane Austen, *Northanger Abbey*, 1798, Harmondsworth, Penguin edition 1994, p. 148.

71 *Ibid.*, p. 146.

72 Illustrated in Arnold, *Patterns*, p. 8.

73 Illustrated in *ibid.*, p. 46.

74 *British Sporting Painting*, cat. No. 149.

75 Cited in Arnold, *Patterns*, pp. 11–13.

76 Illustrated in *ibid.*, p. 12.

77 Illustrated in colour in Jane Dorner, *Fashion*, 1974, p. 38.

78 Philadelphia Museum of Fine Art, publication of drawings, pattern and details, forthcoming.

79 For example, Museum of London, navy cloth habit *c.* 1855, acc. no. 53–49/2; Gallery of English Costume, Manchester, brown twilled wool habit, *c.* 1880–90,

illustrated in *Gallery of English Costume Picture Book Number Eight: Costume for Sport*, 1963, Manchester, Nos 2 and 3.

80 T. H. Holding, *Direct System of Ladies' Cutting*, 1901, pp. 148–50.

81 Safety train by Mr J. Colin Campbell, *ibid.*, p. 160.

82 *Ibid.*, p. 126.

83 George W. Clarke's safety habit skirt, *ibid.*, pp. 155–7.

84 *Ibid.*, p. 157.

3 ✧ Wool cloth and gender: the use of woollen cloth in women's dress in Britain, 1865–85 [1]

Lou Taylor

Introduction

THIS study examines the design development of heavyweight woollen fashion fabric used in the new tailored outdoor garments for middle- and upper-class women's wear in Britain in the 1865–85 period.

Usefully for this study, material cultural approaches to objects now accept Daniel Miller's belief in 'consumption as the vanguard of history'.[2] Ann Smart Martin argues in addition that the material objects of consumption 'matter because they are complex, symbolic bundles of social, cultural and individual meanings fused onto something we can touch, see and own. That very quality is the reason that social values can so quickly penetrate into and evaporate out of common objects'.[3] The design, manufacture and consumption of dress and fashion fabrics of the eighteenth century has already been set within the Miller/Smart Martin framework. Researchers such as Styles, Vickery, Lemire and Ellis Miller have found this methodology to be a valuable vehicle through which to articulate significant debate about the social and economic consequences of growing consumer demand in Britain during the 1750–1800 period.[4] However, there has been, as yet, little focus upon the development of new fashion fabrics in the mid to late nineteenth century as a consequence of new consumer demands.

This study intends to show that as women's tailored garments were developed in the 1865–85 period, a new type of woven cloth had also to be created. Thus it was not only the cut and style of these clothes, favoured as they were by respectable upper- and middle-class women consumers, which had to be feminised, but also the fabrics.

Victoria de Grazia writes that 'historians of consumer society still have a formidable task before them: to link particular acts of consumption to collective patterns and to examine these within the broader play of needs, expectations and entitlements specific to different societies'.[5] Analysis of the hitherto often neglected area of the design, manufacture and consumption of mid-to-late nineteenth-century fashion fabrics can progress debate on the concerns of Smart Martin and de Grazia, placing these pioneering fabrics and garments into the existing socio-cultural context of the emergence of the New Woman. This has been amply documented by Barbara Caine, Stella Mary Newton, Leonora Davidoff and Sheila Rowbotham among others.[6]

Outdoor clothing for upper- and middle-class women in the 1860s

The advent of tailored costumes and more practical clothing for middle- and upper-class women was not a sudden development invented, as many dress histories imply, by the dress reform movements in the 1880s. The roots are far older. Wealthy women had been wearing personally fitted, tailored, woollen riding habits made by their husbands' tailors certainly from the seventeenth century. This tradition continued right through the nineteenth century, famously in Britain. In 1851, Hyam, Tailor and National Clothier of Manchester and London, for example, offered bespoke and ready-to-wear habits 'matchless in price and make; the materials have been selected from the first houses in England and Scotland and possess important requisites for sporting and ordinary walking purposes'. Prices ran from fifty to a hundred shillings.[7] Normal outdoor wear, which by the 1850s and 1860s had to go over massively full skirts and hoops, consisted of quilted silk capes wadded with cotton fluff, large, lightweight wool shawls, hooded burnouses and cloaks and mantles. These came in a range of fabrics, from transparent silk gauze, through lightweight wool, to luxurious heavy silk velvets.

These loose outdoor garments were easily made up by the burgeoning ready-to-wear companies for the growing, fashion-aware, middle-class, feminine consumer market. *The Queen* on 31 May 1862, for example, featured an H. J. and D. Nicholl's advertisement announcing that 'the Burnous and paletots are kept ready in great variety for inspection or use'. More radically functional outdoor styles gradually began to appear in winter-weight mantles, and travelling clothes. By the late 1860s we see the development of 'waterproofs', so-called in both France and England. These seem to have been accepted with little social comment and were simply worn as a protection over the top of normal fashionable dress. They were strikingly plain and serviceable. *La Mode Illustrée* of 2 April 1876, featured two such 'waterproofs', from the smart Parisian dressmaker Mme Fladry, cut large enough to go over bustle-backed dresses. They were of seven–eighths length, with very deep and wide sleeves and large serviceable buttons (figure 10).

Practical, warm and serviceable jackets were another major design breakthrough in the early 1860s still often only partly fitted to allow for the huge skirt worn beneath. The Scotch Tweed Cloak Warehouse in

10   Waterproof by Mme Maury, Paris, *La Mode Illustrée*, June 1875

Piccadilly announced in *The Queen* of 12 December 1863, the availability of their 'Ladies and Gentlemen's ready-made yachting, walking and riding jackets, cloaks, paletots, in linsey-woolsey'.

During the 1860s, upper- and middle-class women became more physically active. As well as horse riding, croquet, archery, tennis and walking were all practised by respectable women. Thus countryside walking, touring in Scotland (following Queen Victoria's example) and in Austria, Switzerland, Italy and indeed in more exotic destinations such as the Middle East, were all considered increasingly acceptable throughout the 1870s and 1880s. All this was made easier by the new railway and steam ship companies and travel agencies such as Thomas Cook.

This public, physical, feminine activity inevitably raised considerations of what was considered sartorially 'suitable,' creating a new set of etiquette problems for women. These problems were not confined to progressive circles only. Even the socially conventional journal, *The Queen*, on 18 July 1863 reported a comment made during a debate at the annual Social Science Congress attended by health reformers of both sexes, which stated that 'we can do many things, but we cannot find a suitable dress even for

6 months and the same shape of coat or of a dress or bonnet will never serve for 2 seasons … The ladies' dress of the present day is … proof against all the shafts of ridicule'.

The late 1860s: the first stages of the development

This growing consumer interest in more functional clothes was largely resolved by the development of tailor-made garments made specifically for women. These developed slowly from the late 1860s through the usual source of new fashions, the grand salons and fashion houses of Paris. Influences on styles and methods of manufacture were heavily reliant on adapting the functionality of men's military and informal leisure wear. The monthly Paris fashion journal, *La Mode Illustrée*, had no images of women in fitted tailored clothes much before January 1869, when it proposed the latest styles in costumes for street wear. These included 'military tailored jackets for young girls. A very pretty model is … a jacket of gendarme-blue cloth, trimmed with a small standing up collar and facings embroidered with silver; others, more simple, are of navy-blue military cloth faced with dark-blue velvet'.

The tailoring techniques of cutting, shaping and making up such garments were very different from those of dressmakers working with silk, fine wool cloth and cottons/linens. Using heavy wool cloth, the specific skills of the expert tailor were required, such as cutting, fitting, interlining, wadding, stab stitching and the shaping and steaming of sewn cloth with heavy heated irons and so on. At the same time, the tailor still had to take care that his styles responded to the established etiquette codes of the period in order that they should be acceptable to his middle- and upper-class conventional clients.

Thus garments had to take on seasonal fashion styles, such as the changing shape of *tournures* and trains. By the late 1860s, skirts were made in two lengths. The first was the new, informal, *round* skirt, just reaching to the floor but with an even hem. This was worn in the mornings, at home and for croquet, archery and when travelling. In shooting dress, this could even be shortened to the ankle. The second hem length, worn for more formal morning and afternoon functions, was trained. Thus *costume du voyage* and *costume du campagne* had round hems, while promenade dresses were trained (figure 11).

The cut of womens' tailored garments

Long experience of making up women's riding habits was the basis upon which tailors developed these new styles, although there were growing

11 French promenade costume with kilted train (front and back), *La Mode Illustrée*, August 1878

tensions between the need for proper fit and demands for comfort. *The Queen* featured an article on riding habits on 15 November 1862 which, significantly, supported 'sensible women' who preferred a 'sense of freedom and the greater promptitude of action they allow' to those who opted for a 'perfect unwrinkled fit of their habit bodies'. John Thomson, in his treatise *The Art of Tailoring* of about 1886, explained that 'you must be careful not to pinch (the riding habit) too tight across the chest. Some ladies must have them tight all over, but the majority of my lady customers like them a little easy over the chest and as tight as you like at the waist, so as to show off their graceful figures to the very best advantage'.[8]

The English origin of the new tailored garments was acknowledged, especially the development of these styles by famous English tailoring houses. Charles Creed had opened his in Paris as early as 1850. Charles Poynter opened the Paris branch of Redfern in 1881. This English company had

colour plate 1 Pamela Milligan, archivist at the Scottish College of Textiles, with R. and A. Anderson 1852 volume, (no. 1852/53) showing shawl fabrics

colour plate 2 Sample page from pattern book, *French Patterns*, no. 1887, 1/1/20 R. and A. Anderson, 1887, 1/1/20

colour plate 3 Sample of gilt-metal threaded wool novelty cloth from pattern book, *French Patterns*, no. 1887, 1/1/20 R. and A. Anderson, 1887, 1/1/20

been founded in 1842, and by 1891 had a Parisian staff of five hundred.[9] *La Mode de Paris* even declared on 8 February 1885 that it was unpatriotic for fashionable French women to wear such garments 'because all the famous tailors, together with their fabrics, come from the banks of the Thames'.[10]

By the 1870s tailored designs from Paris, however, were being widely copied. The grand London department store Debenham and Freebody, for example, produced a special mail-order catalogue in Autumn 1874 directed at American visitors to London. It stressed Paris, not London, as the one status-giving style source, declaring that 'a Branch House in Paris keeps the Mantle, Costume and Millinery Departments constantly supplied with every Parisian Novelty as it leaves the 'Ateliers' of the various directors of French fashion – while a complete organization at home reproduces the various Models in identically the same materials'.[11]

A search through journals such as *The Queen*, *La Mode Illustreé*, *The Young Ladies Journal* and *La Mode Pratique* shows that the 1874–78 period marked a major development in the design, manufacture and consumption of various tailored jackets, walking costumes and ranges of full-length coats. That this moment also coincided with the introduction of the darted *cuirasse* bodice and the seal-like, waistless princess line, both proposed by Charles Worth in Paris, was no coincidence.

The new garments

The new garments deliberately retained a masculine mood through military-style collars and trimmings, Austro-Hungarian fancy braiding, standing collars and large, functional (male) flap pocket designs (figure 12). The *Young Ladies Journal*, 1 July 1881, reported with surprise that the vogue had lasted so long and that 'tailors are still making cloth jackets for ladies ... The more eccentric have a turned-up military collar, embroidered in gold and facings embroidered in the same style as well as the rounded pockets'. On 1 November 1881, the same journal commented: 'it is to be remarked that the stitched bindings such as are put on to gentlemen's clothes, have now superseded pipings for ladies costumes'.

The 1874 Debenham and Freebody catalogue offered their 'Tweed Costume', which consisted of a jacket, a masculine-styled waistcoat, tunic and skirt and cost £5 5s. These plainish cloth garments were in stark contrast to high-fashion outer garments for day and evening wear, such as a heavy-ribbed, half-length silk paletot, featured in *La Mode Illustrée*, 5 November 1876 and worn over a pronounced bustle. This had fancy fur edging, heavy fringes and complex appliqued embroidery. Others had chiffon and beaded trimmings, complex fish-tail peplums and dangling streamers.

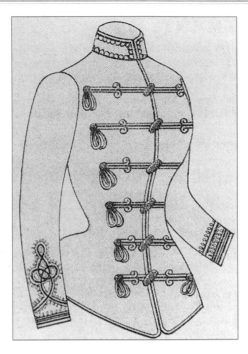

12 James Thomson, *The Ladies Jacket, Ulster and Costume Cutter,* John Williamson, London, n.d. (*c.* 1886): *Ladies Braided Military Jacket*

facing **13** James Thomson, *The Ladies Jacket, Ulster and Costume Cutter,* John Williamson, London, n.d. (*c.* 1886): the *Tyndale Mantle* (left), the *Florence Sling Dolman* (centre) and the *Glencarty Mantle* (right)

Developments in the 1880s

Despite the revival of massive bustles, a steady consolidation of these now feminised tailored garments took place through the 1880s. Demand across the middle and upper classes evidently grew. In about 1885, John Williamson and Company, a large firm based in Drury Lane, London, which provided paper patterns for tailored garments to order for private, bespoke and wholesale work, expanded their Ladies Department. They declared this to 'have been very successful ... we are still further improving and developing, so as to lay before the trade periodical patterns of great variety in style and perfection in fit'.[12] By the mid-1880s, standard, fully tailored garments for women as listed by James Thomson, included riding habits, ladies covert coats, ulsters, chesterfield and Norfolk jackets, military jackets, cloaks, dolmans and capes, many keeping their original masculine names (figure 13).

Fabrics: 1850–90

Gender diversity in mid-nineteenth-century wool cloth is clear. Men wore tougher, rougher, heavier and darker woollen cloth. Women wore lighter-weight, fancier, wool fabrics for dresses and shawls. The fashion fabric industries of France and Britain had reached very sophisticated levels of

product diversity by the middle of the century in response to the rapidly increasing demands of male and female middle-class consumers. Research into mourning fabrics for women, to give just one example, revealed that as the cult of mourning built up through the century, forty-nine different types of black mourning fabric, from expensive silk and wool to the cheapest cotton, were on sale in Britain by 1900.[13]

The Scottish College of Textiles in Galashiels, Scotland, holds a fascinating collection of sample books from local mills which verify that the Scottish Border cloth manufacture in this period was weighted heavily towards menswear fabrics, producing only a few ranges of women's cloth. The sample books of R. and A. Anderson,[14] through the 1850s to 1880s, show many hundreds of examples of gendered woollen cloth. This company, like all the others in the Borders, specialised in classic male suitings and coatings in Border, district, gun club, shepherd checks and tweeds and lovats, worn for informal urban and rural leisure wear. The firm also wove special Border check plaids (large shawls) worn functionally in inclement weather by shepherds.[15] A sample book of 1852 [16] features small samples of heavy-weight trouser cloth, each with its own side-seam stripe woven into the cloth, as well as examples of small and large checks and lovat cloths. Colours, though surprisingly and delicately variegated, are distinctly dark, with only some waistcoatings in paler tones. All these cloths are heavy and designed for making up by tailoring methods. T. A. Stillie explains that by 1850 weights of cloth varied from '28 ozs. for Cheviots to 13–14 ozs for Saxonies,'[17] the latter being used for 'women's shirtings'.

However, R. and A. Anderson, like other Border mills, also made even lighter-weight tartan wool cloth for shawls and possibly for ladies' dresses, woven in the boldest and brightest of large-patterned tartans in reds, oranges, deep pinks, greens and blues (colour plate 1). Kenneth Ponting confirms that examples of such Border cloths were shown at the 1851 Great Exhibition. These included 'the hunting Macdonald tartan and fabric for ladies dresses made of Saxony lamb's wools' exhibited by Robert Gill of Innerleithen and Ladies Scotch Plaids' by James Sime of Galashiels.[18] The gendered difference here is clear. Stillie identifies the weight of women's shawl cloths to be 'as low as 10 oz'. Cheviots for menswear at 28 ozs were therefore nearly three times this weight. When shawls went out of fashion in the late 1870s, this cloth 'ceased to be of any consequence' in Border manufacture, while 'the tweed and heavy woollens continued to expand'.[19]

Once female consumer interest in tailor-made clothes had been established, the problem of gender suitability of fabric reared its head. The finer wool fabrics were simply not sturdy enough while the standard male cloths of the late 1860s, such as the serviceable tweeds and serges of R. and A. Anderson, epitomised familiar representations of Victorian masculinity. In strong, dark and earthy colours, these were the absolute and deliberate antithesis to notions of conventional sartorial femininity associated with lace, fine silks, delicate appliqués, soft, or light fabrics, as John Harvey has so eruditely explained.[20]

This gendered view of male cloth remained in place until, and indeed beyond, the end of the century, as is perfectly indicated in Grant Allen's 1895 novel *The Woman Who Did*. The heroine's daughter, brought up by her radical mother who wore aesthetic dress, finally gets to meet upper-class Englishmen on a visit to a grand country estate.

> For the first time in life she saw something of men, real men, with horses and dogs and guns – men who went out partridge shooting in the season and rode to hounds across country, not the pale abstractions of cultured humanity who attended Fabian society meetings or wrote things called articles in the London papers. Her mother's friends wore soft felt hats and limp woollen collars; these real men were richly clad in tweed suits and fine linen.[21]

Fabric development in the 1880s

So if tweeds and country checks were so masculine, what was to be done about providing women consumers with more 'suitable' fabrics for their new garments? Some fashion plates dating from the late 1860s to the early

14 Travelling coat, Paris, *La Mode Illustrée*, April 1875

15 Travelling costume, fashion plate from *Le Journal des Modes*, *c.*1882

1880s indicate that sometimes nothing at all was done and that men's fabrics were used directly by women (figure 14). The consequences were not always happy. Whereas a big, bold check might look handsome made up into a large and loose informal overcoat for a man, on a woman the results could be less than beautiful. A slim travelling costume from *Journal des Modes* of about 1882 (figure 15) was designed in the boldest of masculine-looking checked cloth. The checks are cut up by the princess line bodice seaming in a curiously unflattering manner. This plate's dull, drab, beige colours were also masculine in taste but the *Textile Manufacturer* reporting on the latest menswear fabrics from Huddersfield in 1877, declared that 'it may be stated that the prevailing features are checks and plaids,' and that 'the same style of ornamentation appears in cloths for ladies wear, the colours of which are often delicate shades of drab'.[22]

There is no doubt that the masculine character of such fabrics was still in place in the 1880s. Thus *The Young Ladies Journal*, 1 November

1881, vaunted the popularity of material for winter costumes in 'Cheviot cloths in tiny checks or thread stripes'.[23] However, more acceptable womanly coding soon became evident. *The Delineator*, 15 December 1884,[24] favoured the adoption of male patterns by women provided they were feminised.

> To take without asking, the fabrics usually dedicated to the masculine world, to improve upon them and then to ask if they are not becoming, is what womankind has done lately. And the result is more than satisfactory – to one part of the world at least. Wool suitings, following in colours and design just such effects as men favour, but made somewhat lighter in weight – wherein lies the only difference – are much favoured for walking costumes. They are very wide, claiming 50 inches, and, while sometimes they seem costly, their great width is really full compensation. A fine check in white and yellow upon brown and a black dotted with dark blue and having squares of scarlet outlined upon it to produce a plaid effect, gives a very good idea of these essentially quiet and yet becoming fabrics.

Clearly styling had moved on from figure 15, whose bold check is very far from 'quiet'.

This eager interest in heavier fashion cloths was soon met by commercially aware manufacturers. The *World of Fashion*, November 1884, declared that a plain rough serge, neatly braided, makes a useful 'knock-about' dress for town or country wear. In the same month *The Ladies Treasury* confirmed that 'rough fabrics are especially chosen for making up confections of every kind, thus rendering the till now fashionable wadded and quilted linings unnecessary'.[25]

The latter comment serves to remind us of the modernity of these new cloths. They replaced the complexities of layered interlinings and waddings of cotton fluff which dressmakers had previously used to keep their customers warm. The *World of Fashion* reported in December of 1884 that 'ladies are beginning to recognise the comfort of a good real woollen dress, made from a fabric of weight, which suits itself to the modern requirements of draping and kilting with grace and adaptability, and which above all looks well and ladylike on any occasion for day wear'.[26] By the summer of 1887, *Sylvia's Home Journal* was pointing out the pleasures of wearing woollen tailor-mades in light tweeds and cashmeres 'without additional covering out of doors'.[27]

Thus, fashion journal comments on suitable woollen fabric increased from year to year, as did the variety and novelty of the cloth. The *World of Fashion*, November 1884, proposed the use of plain materials accompanied by matching, checked 'cheviots and rough-finished flannels' suggesting that these were perfect for wearers 'meant to take long tramps to give their cheeks a glow'.[28]

Novelty cloths

Trade journals, fashion magazines, tailoring books and surviving garments and samples all show that by the 1880s cloth manufacturers had successfully altered the feel of the cloth from a rough to a softer touch. Cloths became somewhat lighter in weight and much more elaborate, with bouclé, mate-lassée, corded and even astrakhan-type finishes. These novelty fabrics can all be seen in a fascinating sample book in the R. and A. Anderson archives in Galashiels, clearly dated and labelled 'French Patterns, 1887' [29] (colour plate 2).

Fabric colours were rapidly feminised too by linking them into the existing system of seasonal colour and texture change which was diffused internationally from Paris. The 1874 Debenham and Freebody catalogue lists a complete range of Paris-derived colours for that autumn's tailored garments, 'mostly dark in tone, including Marron, Choco, the new Damson Blue, five shades of Claret, two of Heliotrope and fashionable Fraises Ecrasées'. By 1885, the *Textile Recorder* in its monthly fashion forecasting column 'Fashionable Materials' noted that the *World of Fashion* of February of that year proposed plain, winter, cloth colours of 'brown, navy blue, olive-green, myrtle green and the numerous shades of red'. These deep and rich colours are also all clearly still evident in the R. and A. Anderson 1887 'French Pattern' sample book, where claret, deep yellow-ochre, browns and myrtle greens still predominate.

Consumers seemed to have responded well and manufacturers, conti-nued to develop ever more innovative, novelty yardage. Fashion journals promoted them too, though still finding it necessary to explain their correct etiquette use. Thus *Myra's Journal of Dress and Fashion*, December 1884,[30] noted that:

> new materials are still appearing, and base their well-deserved claims to novelty on their names and texture, while it may be safely predicted that the costumes composed of them will be in the highest degree typical and stylish. *Bouclette Tibet* is a rough, ribbed, hairy fabric, with an indefinable pattern and in the newest shades – this will be used only for walking costumes; *paillasson*, a kind of thick, supple armure, with a raised pattern in the style of *oatmeal cloth* will be used for the same purpose.

In November of 1884, the *World of Fashion* commented that 'the new serge, which is striped with silver or steel threads, when suitably trimmed with rich fancy braid and garnished with lace, is quite handsome enough for a visiting or reception dress. Many of the new Bradford serges have a wide ribbon border of metal threads in steel, gold or silver ... these are very effective and are purely of home manufacture'.[31] Only two months later the *Ladies Treasury*, January 1885, noted, however, that fashion fabrics containing gold and silver threads within their weave were 'losing their popularity for walking costumes ... because they tarnish when exposed to the air and lose all their fascinating glitter'.[32] As befits fabric for day wear, the metal glint was of the utmost discretion. Pamela Milligan, the archivist of the textile collection at the Scottish College of Textiles, Galashiels, spotted a sample of exactly this gilt-threaded fabric in the 1887 R. and A. Anderson 'French Patterns' sample book, so evidently these fabrics were not exclusive to Bradford and did in fact remain fashionable for at least two more years (colour plate 3).

'Woollen Snow' was another novelty wool texture, highlighted in the December 1884 edition of *The Ladies Treasury*. The fabric was named as 'the newest material-woollen plush ... which looks like frosted worsted'.[33] The *Kensington and Hammersmith Times*, 13 September 1884, focused on yet another new line. 'Among the new winter materials which have just appeared in Paris are woollen reps with a very thick cords ... like chenille, at intervals. Some have the cords crossed at intervals by a silk stitch, something like couching'. *Bison cloth* was a gimmick novelty in 1884. 'Our Ladies Column' in the *Kensington and Hammersmith Times* reported on 13 September that it gave 'an undressed appearance giving a semi-civilised style,' with its 'ground of long haired thick cords'. *The Ladies Treasury* passed a more favourable eye on the same fabric, providing its use involved no breaking of feminine etiquette codes. 'A great preference is shown for very coarse woollen fabrics some of which is quite canvas like with short hairs covering the surface, and naturally are only employed for morning wear.'[34]

The R. and A. Anderson 1887 'French Patterns' volume also contains many pretty examples of wool cloth spotted with sheeny silk yarns or furred discreetly with the raised pile of silk chenille threads. These were also featured in the December 1884 edition of the *World of Fashion*. 'The figured woollens are really very elegant, pretty patterns being raised on the plain surface in silk, satin or chenille spots.' In the same month, *Myra's Journal of Dress and Fashion* noted that the new 'cheviots embroidered with chenille are employed for more elegant walking costumes' and that 'when tastefully combined with plain fabric to match, it is impossible to imagine a more thoroughly satisfactory costume than is supplied by English Woollens'.[35]

It seems, despite the evident consumer interest in novelty cloths, that the 'French Patterns' samples had no dramatic impact on the design and technology of R. and D. Anderson's products. Ken Ponting points out that the Border textile trade made only very limited adaptions to existing masculine lines. Some reversible coatings such as styles checked on one side and plain on the other were recoloured to shades of light blue and camel tones 'for ladies' mantles'. Overall, the Borders, like the west of England, 'failed to capture a section of this new ladies' trade, which was developing fast ... another sign of that area's failure to grasp opportunities offered'.[36] T. A. Stillie agreed that the Scottish Border trade was almost wholly in gents' wear and only a few select companies dealt in ladies' wear ... often through sportswear cloths designed for the gents' trade'.[37] According to Dr J. G. Martindale, the Principal of the Scottish Woollen Technical College Galashiels (now the Scottish College of Textiles), it was not until about 1930 that the Border trade 'began to display a great interest in ladies' wear'.[38]

Instead, the new, woollen fashion fabrics were imported into Britain from France and were woven in English mills in the Huddersfield, Leeds and Halifax industries. In 1877 the *Textile Manufacturer* noted that the colours of Huddersfield worsted coatings for that year were 'usually black or blue with a check or diamond pattern ... and the same style of ornamentation appears in cloths for ladies' wear'.[39] On 10 December 1877, the journal's special correspondent from Leeds noted that the slow demand for spring coatings had been alleviated a little because 'the fashionable dressmakers have improved trade somewhat by fostering a taste for various cloths for ladies' clothing and this class of goods has been freely pur-chased'.[40]

Conclusion

Feminine tailored fabrics and garments, whether made in France or England, were for many years inevitably tagged with the derogatory label of 'mas-culine' because of the cut, making-up methods, cloth design and cultural coding that were their root base. The hostile comments started at once in a manner already familiar to campaigners who had earlier attempted to wear the bloomer costume. A cartoon in *The Queen*, 7 February 1863, featured a woman in an early form of tailored *redingote* being accused of looking no different from a footman in livery or a soldier in regimental uniform.

However, the push for practical, feminine, activity clothing was irre-versible. Thus Dudley's Mart, a wholesale, ready-to-wear, tailored garment manufacturer with outlets spread from Birmingham to Newport and Luton, in about 1885, offered elegant, tailored, bustle-backed paletot coats, in 'plush, silks, cloth of all kinds, trimmed with Russian fur'[41] aimed towards a middle-class clientele (figure 16). Ten years later these styles were being mass produced, in a process described by dress historians as the demo-cratisation of fashion. In 1896, the much advertised 10/6d John Noble

16 Check cloth paletot from Dudley's Mart catalogue *c.*1885

Half-Guinea Costume in 'John Noble Cheviot serge' could be bought in a colour range running from black, grey, navy, brown, myrtle, to electric blue, petunia and ruby. This, along with other similar styles, was marketed as 'suitable for Morning or General Wear, Gardening, Walking, Climbing, Boating, Tennis, Travelling or, in fact, for Any Wear or Anywearer Anywhere'.[42] More elegant garments from this period have survived, such as a French example from the Palais Galliera's collection, a black tailored costume of 1890–92 trimmed with black velvet on the collar and centre front.[43] The Platt Hall Gallery of Costume in Manchester owns a splendid purple walking costume of 1898, also with matching velvet trim on its jacket.

This object-based research confirms that a process of feminisation of male wool cloth took place over the 1865–85 period as a result of a growing consumer demand by well-off women for more practical tailored dress. This indicates that the dress reform movement, which reached a peak of activity in Britain in the 1883–1900 period, built upon, rather than created, the success of already established tailored styles. The sartorial radicalism within the movement lay therefore not in the use of heavier weight woolcloth but rather in its campaigns for ever more rationalism in tailored styles; in its campaigning for the social acceptance of bifurcated garments worn by women; and finally, in its proposals that women should have the right to wear these modern styles when and where they wanted to.

The development of the fabrics described here was fundamental to all of this. These cloths represented a new image of progressive, feminine, modernity. It is only when cloth structure, feel, weight, colour, end use and consumer market, as well as the relationship to Paris-based styling and society etiquette codes, are all set in place that the full cultural biography of these materials can be properly drawn up. To this end, a multi- disciplinary approach, aiming to satisfy de Grazia's 'broader play of needs, expectations and entitlements,' helps to clarify the radically-gendered modernity of both these fabrics and the tailored garments made from them.

Notes

1 With many thanks to Mary Schoeser for the initial introduction and to Pamela Milligan, Archivist of the Historical Textiles and Business Records at the Scottish College of Textiles, Galashiels.

2 Daniel Miller, *Acknowledging Consumption, A Review of New Studies*, London, Routledge, 1995, pp. 1–57.

3 Ann Smart Martin, *Makers, Buyers and Users – Consumerism as a Material Culture Framework*, Winterthur Portfolio, 28 (2/4), summer/autumn 1993, p. 14.

4 See Daniel Roche, *Culture of Clothing: Dress and Fashion in the Ancien Régime*, Cambridge, Cambridge University Press, 1994; Lesley Ellis Miller, *Designers in the Lyons Silk Industry, 1712–1787*, Ph.D. thesis, University of Brighton, 1988; 'Dressing Down in 18th-Century France: The Clothing of Silk Designers', *Costume*, no. 29, 1995; Roy Porter, *The Consumption of Culture 1600–1800 – Image, Object, Text*, London, Routledge, 1995; Natalie Rothstein, *Barbara Johnson's Album of Fashion and Fabrics*, London, Thames and Hudson, 1990; see also Amanda Vickery, 'Mrs Shackelton's Wardrobe and John Styles, Manufacturing, Consumption and Design in 18th-Century England', in J. Brewer and R. Porter, *Consumption and the World of Goods*, London, Routledge, 1993; Beverly Lemire, *Fashion's Favourite: The Cotton Trade and the Consumer in Britain, 1660–1800*, Oxford, Oxford University Press, 1991.

5 Victoria de Grazia (ed.), *The Sex of Things, Gender and Consumption in Historical Perspective*, Berkeley, University of California Press, 1996, p. 279.

6 See Barbara Caine, *Victorian Feminists*, Oxford, Oxford University Press, 1992; Leonora Davidoff, *The Best Circles*, London, Croom Helm, 1973; Juliet Gardiner (ed.), *The New Woman: Womens' Voices – 1880–1913*, London, Collins and Brown, 1993; Stella Mary Newton, *Health, Art and Reason*, London, John Murray, 1974; Sheila Rowbotham, *Women in Movement – Feminism and Social Action*, London, Routledge, 1992.

7 Hyam, Tailor and National Clothier, catalogue, n.d. but published to coincide with the Great Exhibition of 1851. Author's collection. This large-scale manufacturer already had outlets in cities including London, Manchester, Liverpool, Birmingham, Bristol, Dublin and Glasgow.

8 James Thomson, 'The Ladies Jacket, Ulster and Costume Cutter, embracing all the

new and popular styles of tailor-made garments', London, John Williamson, n.d. but about 1886 (with thanks to Suzanne Davies).

9   Anny Latour, *Kings of Fashion*, London, Weidenfeld & Nicolson, 1958, p. 131.

10 Renée Davray-Piekolek, 'Les Modes Triomphantes, 1885–1895', in Musée de la Mode et du Costume, Palais Galliera, *Femmes Fin de Siècle: 1885–1895*, Paris, Paris-Musées, 1990, p. 45.

11 Debenham and Freebody, Dry Goods Store, *The New Fashion Book, Autumn 1874*, with thanks to Sarah Johnson, who found this catalogue in the archives of the Winterthur Museum collection, Delaware, USA.

12 John Thomson, 'The Ladies Jacket, Ulster and Costume Cutter', advertisement for John Williamson, 93/94 Drury Lane, London, model and special pattern department.

13 Lou Taylor, *Mourning Dress, a Costume and Social History*, London, Allen and Unwin, 1983, Appendix 1, pp. 288–301.

14 R. and A. Anderson's, with a specialism in cloth for men's wear, was founded in 1832 by Robert and Alexander Anderson at the Gala Mill Galashiels and functioned until 1957. See *Galashiels, a Modern History*, Galashiels History Committee and Ettrick and Lauderdale District Council, Galashiels, 1983, p. 69.

15 For details on such designs see E. S. Harrison, *Our Scottish District Checks*, Edinburgh, National Association of Scottish Woollen Manufacturers, 1968.

16 R. and A. Anderson archives, no. 1852/53, Archive of Historical Records and Business Archives, the Scottish College of Textiles, Galashiels.

17 T. A. Stillie, 'The Evolution of Pattern Design in the Scottish Woollen Textile Industry in the Nineteenth Century', *Textile History*, Vol. 1, Newton Abbot, David and Charles, 1971, pp. 321, 324.

18 Kenneth Ponting, 'The Scottish Contribution to Wool Textile Design in the Nineteenth Century', p. 89, in John Butt and Kenneth Ponting, *Scottish Textile History*, Aberdeen, Aberdeen University Press, 1987.

19 T. A. Stillie, 'Evolution of Pattern Design', p. 322.

20 See John Harvey, *Men in Black*, London, Reaktion, 1995.

21 Grant Allen, *The Woman Who Did*, London, John Lane, 1895, p. 208.

22 *Textile Manufacturer*, 15 June 1877, p. 186.

23 *Textile Recorder*, 'Fashionable Materials', 15 November 1881 and 15 February 1881.

24 *Ibid.*, 15 December 1884, p. 186.

25 *Ibid.*, 15 November 1884, p. 164.

26 *Ibid.*, 15 December 1884, p. 186.

27 *Ibid.*, 14 May 1887.

28 *Ibid.*, 15 November 1884, p. 164.

29 The R. and A. Anderson Archives at the Scottish College of Textiles at Galashiels have two volumes dated 1887, 'French Patterns'. Comparison with other volumes (1852–90) show these to contain samples which are markedly different from the firm's usual styles of menswear cloth. This research indicates that these are indeed French samples of fashionable wool cloth for an élite feminine market probably taken to the R. and A. Anderson mill for closer analysis. The fabrics glued into the 1887 volume are astonishing in their technical complexity and variety and their very close similarity to the high fashion French and English woollen cloths described

here and seen in corresponding colours in period fashion plates. (With many thanks to Pamela Milligan, Archivist at the Scottish College of Textiles Galashiels, for her patience and help in discussing these volumes and for permission to use photographs.)

30 *Textile Recorder*, 'Fashionable Materials', 15 December 1884, p. 186.

31 *Ibid.*, 15 November 1884, p. 164.

32 *Ibid.*, 15 January 1885, p. 210.

33 *Ibid.*, 15 December 1884, p. 186.

34 *Ibid.*, 15 November 1884, p. 164.

35 *Ibid.*, 15 December 1884, p. 186.

36 Ponting, 'Scottish Contribution', p. 85.

37 T. A. Stillie, 'Evolution of Pattern Design', p. 331.

38 The Wool Education Society, 'The Scottish Woollen Industry', a lecture by J. G. Martindale at the Royal Society of Arts, 23 February 1954, The Department of Education of the International Wool Secretariat, London, 1954.

39 *Textile Manufacturer*, 15 June 1877, p. 186.

40 *Ibid.*, 10 December 1877, p. 397.

41 Dudley's Mart, 45 and 47, London Road, Liverpool, Manufactory for Mantles, Costumes, Millinery Furs etc., catalogue, *c.* 1885. (With thanks to Suzanne Davies.)

42 *The Lady's Companion*, 19 September 1896, p. 383, advertisement for 'The John Noble Model Costumes' author's collection.

43 Musée de la Mode et du Costume, Palais Galliera, *Femmes Fin de Siècle: 1885–1895*, Paris-Musées, 1990, p. 164, a black wool cloth costume of 1890–92, (no. 60.9.2) and Plate 20, a purple wool cloth walking costume of 1898, in Picture Book no. 5, Gallery of English Costume, Manchester, 1953.

4 ✧ Renouncing consumption: men, fashion and luxury, 1870–1914

Christopher Breward

Conceive me, if you can
An everyday young man:
A commonplace type,
With a stick and a pipe,
And a half bred black and tan;
Who thinks suburban 'hops'
More fun than 'Monday Pops',
Who's fond of his dinner
And doesn't get thinner
On bottled beer and chops.   (Gilbert and Sullivan, *Patience*)

A T the climax of Gilbert and Sullivan's *Patience*, the comic opera conceived as a parody of the pretensions of the aesthetic movement, and promoted in America during 1881 through a lecture tour fronted by Oscar Wilde himself, the poet Grosvenor rejects the dirty greens and lank limbs of Bohemia for the brash and hearty world of convention. Much has been made of the manner in which Wilde's connections with the opera established him both as a public icon of artistic unconventionality and as an embodiment of those associated debates revolving around standards of masculine respectability and the broader effects of capitalism on acceptable modes for the manly. Fourteen years later, at Wilde's trial, those visual and lyrical references mooted in *Patience* resurfaced in a more aggressive demonstration of the permissible and the forbidden in terms of male behaviour and image. Wilde's manipulation of appearances and use of clothing as an oppositional tool have indeed been used since that event to illustrate the emergence of the effeminate dandy as a cipher for modern homosexuality, a marker against which gendered identities have been judged and assessed.[1] Indeed, the history of male clothing in the nineteenth century has been explained away largely as a phenomenon of denial related directly to, and mirror imaging, the oppositional posturing of the dandy.[2] What of that other figure conjured up in Gilbert's libretto though, whose unspectacular espousal of the three-penny bus and the ready-made suit, marked him out as a modern icon equally pervasive, though comparatively ignored or taken for granted? When sexual stereotypes are forged and fermented, what happens to the model of the 'everyday young man'?

The final decades of the nineteenth century present a particularly fruitful period for research based around the construction and formation of gendered identities within the market place. They encompass several areas that have been isolated as pivotal moments in a perceived history of 'mass fashion consumption' – the rise of the department store,[3] the establishment of an organised couture and ready-made clothing industry,[4] and the culmination of a system of publicity and advertising that redefined the role played by gender in patterns of dress.[5] However, recent histories of late nineteenth-century consumption have tended to concentrate on the effects any changes might have had on new constructions of metropolitan femininity, or on the allied construction of subversive and élite forms of masculinity.[6] The role of men 'at large' as consumers within this new arena of shopping and acquisition has not yet been studied in its own right, presumably because the majority of men are assumed to have been absent from this particular sphere of activity. In the course of this chapter I therefore propose to suggest ways in which issues of masculinity have been positioned in recent accounts of historical clothing practices, leading towards a tentative discussion of a particular area of late nineteenth-century cultural and material production that describes the problematic position of those lost Victorian men 'who shopped'.

The *Practical Retail Draper*, a commercial guide published in 1912 had the following comments to offer concerning the consumption choices of male consumers:

> There is every reason why men's clothing should be advertised to women, for from the time a boy is born until he is well out of his teens his mother selects all his clothing. After that his sweetheart's taste must be catered for, in that he dresses to please her. Then his wife begins to select his clothing and influences his personal expenditure, so that throughout the lifetime of the average man, women have the controlling voice in the matter of his dress.[7]

Such a rhetoric, with its implication that spending practice lay firmly under the control of women, was typical in its denial of the role played by men in the management and acquisition of clothing. Indeed the proliferation of similar renunciatory accounts in trade periodicals and family literature, alongside a relative lack of empirical evidence regarding men's dress and possessions, offers an initial indication of the reasons for the marginalisation of masculine consumption habits by recent historical enquiry. Undoubtedly it is primarily through the discourse of 'separate spheres', which neatly echoes the polarised nature of much contemporary documentation, that many have attempted to structure and explain the social roles taken by men and women during the nineteenth century, defining the processes of production and consumption as respectively masculine and feminine.[8] Yet while historians have been relatively success-ful in establishing models for new forms of feminine consumption and their representation that fit within a 'separate spheres' paradigm, the repercussions for an understanding of masculinity within the market place are accordingly not so positive. Rarely in the vibrant secondary literature that has developed around issues of nineteenth-century commodity culture over the past ten years is there evidence of any real discussion of actual physical divisions or gender-specific activity in shopping practices beyond the more nebulous act of looking, the relationship between sumptuous shop display and the female gaze, which makes any material quantification of consumption on gendered lines tenuous at the very least.[9] In the words of social historian Nancy Cott, any history aiming to delineate masculine equivalents needs to distinguish between 'what is exclusively male culture and what is public, as the two can no longer be viewed as strictly coterminous'.[10] Taking the lead from recent women's history, the circulation of mythic cultural rhetorics that stressed clear divisions between gendered patterns of social behaviour has to be viewed as distinct from the way that men and women ordered their everyday lives, often in direct contra-diction to prevailing cultural tropes. The language of separate spheres was largely a work of fiction, generated in representational forms by magazine editors, novelists and the authors of etiquette guides. Its simple application to physical sites and fixed identities is now notoriously problematic and in the field of fashion a too literal reading of such controlling devices has succeeded in obscuring actual choice and practice, in women's dress certainly, in men's absolutely.

Having questioned the use of all-encompassing historical explanations of private and public, it may be useful to indicate those broader spaces in which constructions of masculine patterns of consumption and sartorial behaviour defined themselves, extending the challenge to limited positivist readings of Victorian culture, and partially illuminating the particular ways in which urban male consumers intervened in a perceived feminine domain. In the interests of focus, I hope to isolate those sources that describe the consumption practices of one particular social type, the city clerk, who himself crystallised a variety of specifically 'modern' notions of masculinity at the turn of the century, and illustrates the need for a methodological approach that prioritises plurality and choice while recognising the inher-ent tensions between rhetoric and experience. Space does not allow a comprehensive study, but it is hoped that the historical sources utilised will point towards a means of accessing and defining hidden historical fashion practices.

To remain with the role of rhetoric in dictating appearances, a central and sustaining device in terms of the construction of nineteenth-century masculinities was that which stressed the incompatibility between a self-aware enjoyment of leisured shopping or fashionable display and so-called 'traditional' standards of muscular manliness. Samuel Pearson proffering advice in the etiquette guide *Weekday Living – A Book for Young Men and Women* of 1882 recalls how:

> I have sometimes wondered whether men or women were more vain in matters of dress. At certain periods of life it is quite common to see a young fellow strutting along the street as proud as any peacock. The unexceptional attire, from the crown of the hat to the sole of the patent leather boots, the band box associations which clung around the whole get-up, the enormous outlay of starch suggested – these things would be startling if they were not ridiculous.[11]

Yet this condemnation of sartorial excess also contradicts the strong associations demanded in such texts between concepts of manliness and rigid codes of visual respectability. So two pages later, Pearson is falling back on the familiar assumption that men should relinquish sartorial choice to the proper feminine sphere in order to retain the appearance of decorum:

> A young man is looked over and appraised before he can open his lips. If his shirt button is not sewn on, or if his hat is unbrushed, or if he be out at elbows in more senses than one, he may have some immense ability, but he does not get credit for the fact. Why should a man spoil his chances in life for want of a little care?[12]

The relevance of Pearson's strictures regarding clothing and respectability was especially pointed for those recipients of similar rules and prescriptions employed in the rapidly expanding offices and counting rooms of the civil service, the law and the city, concerns which made up the commercial heart of late Victorian London. The world of clerical work has rarely been equated with opportunities for fashionable display, yet titles such as *The Commercial Clerk and his Success*, a career guide published in 1909, reveal a contested field of fraught guidelines and suggestions regarding suitable dress:

> The clerk owes it to his employer to be ever neat and particular as to his personal appearance, not overdressed nor extravagantly attired in any degree, but dressed as though he respects his firm, himself and his calling. To appear

at the office unshaven, or with unbrushed coat and dirty boots, proclaims at once a lack of respect to one's employers and oneself.[13]

The junior clerk in particular, forming part of that large, shifting, single-male population, renting single bedsitters, or frugal boarding-house rooms in the more dingy inner suburbs, faced the material consequences of keeping up appearances on a minimal income, not necessarily anticipated by the writers of helpful self-improvement tracts. Osmond Ormesby, the fictional hero of one of the many popular clerk novels marketed towards young men in the 1880s and 1990s, was typical in having to do without the assistance of female friends and family in creating a sartorial image suited to the rules and rhythms of office life:

> Living on next to nothing a year teaches you what you can do for yourself ... washing is an expensive item in London, especially with regard to collars, and Osmond, who recognised the benefit of a good personal appearance, found himself wearing two or three every week, and thus running up a bill. He discovered that gutta-percha collars could be bought, looking quite as well as those of linen, only possessing much greater advantages. They seldom got dirty, and could be cleaned in a moment with cold water and flannel.[14]

Achieving the appearance of respectability, fashionability even, on a limited budget, inevitably had the effect of exposing those from precarious class backgrounds to the categorising tendencies of late nineteenth-century ethnographical and social discourse, borrowed from the commentaries of imperialist expansion. Denizens of the square mile, alongside the more familiar reports of degenerate East Enders, were constantly scrutinised and deconstructed with a zeal that simultaneously suggests the sinister agenda of eugenicists and the concerned hand-wringing of social reformers. 'Arry, the office boy, was among the urban stereotypes isolated by Edwin Pugh in his touristic impression of London *The City of the World* of 1908:

> His feet are big and clumsy: cheap ill-fitting boots account for that ... One suspects a certain slackness and abrupt bulginess about his sleeves and the legs of his trousers that his joints are disproportionately large ... If his hair is ... dark, then he plasters it down tightly on his scalp to a brilliant sleekness and finishes off his coiffure with a slimy arc upon his forehead ... He is not well dressed, but he is at least decently clad in ready made clothes, or clothes made to measure by some cheap cash tailor. Indeed he reeks of cheapness ... He has suitable clothes for every occasion, even evening clothes sometimes – but they are all of a like shoddy quality, and seem all to have been made for somebody else. And the effect of his big hands and big feet, his stringy sinewy neck, and loosely hung limbs, is to accentuate this distressing element of cheapness and tawdriness.[15]

A more accommodating description by Marcus Fall in *London Town – Sketches of Life and Character* of 1896, reaffirmed common observations regarding the tendency of the clerk towards a make-do approximation of contemporary notions of style, compromised by social expectations and restricted funds:

> The clothes of the bank clerk are neither always new, nor without flaws, but they are well brushed and free from spots and carefully repaired. His means do not allow him to indulge in sartorial luxuries, but he grudges no time to rendering his apparel respectfully neat, and no money to his laundress to ensure the purity of his linen. He is low sized, parts his hair in the middle, and wears a coloured tie when the rules of the bank do not forbid it.[16]

Historical enquiry centred on the cultural formations of masculinity has stressed the pressure which models of ideal manhood placed on Victorian men across the social spectrum, and which, alongside economic factors, may have countered a less complicated relationship with the acquisition and display of fashionable dress. Through recourse to the justifying power of historical precedent, concepts as diverse as the supremacy of male friendship over heterosexual marriage, the spiritual beauty of the exercised male physique, muscular Christian exhortations to celibacy, and crusading concepts of imperial might, could become embedded in popular definitions of manliness through institutions as socially wide ranging as school, church, army and club, through to scout troop, football team, chop house and gin palace.[17] As an example of the way in which the rhetorical devices of masculine discourse were made material, it can be seen that suggestive figures including the knight and the athlete constantly recur as decorative and illustrative motifs in elements of Victorian culture, both high and low, including the trappings and publicity of the men's clothing retail industry. 'The Window Dresser's Diary' published in association with the trade journal *The Outfitter* in 1910, typically advised that for Empire Day, the shopkeeper introduced a 'British Imperial Display – Figures of Britannia and the Colonies. Festival of the Empire should suggest ideas. Great opportunity for Scout costumes, riding breeches, leggings, sailor suits and anything suggesting frontier enterprise'.[18]

The power that such concepts held in maintaining the status quo, both undermined and supported attitudes towards fashionable masculinity, pathologising a dissonant and 'unseemly' personal interest in appearances as evidence of inversion and unmanliness, especially after the sensationalist reporting of the Cleveland Street affair and the Wilde trials of 1889 and 1895.[19] At the same time, ironically, supposedly normative forms of masculinity celebrated a culture of shared power which laid emphasis on the physical body through a rhetoric of sportsmanship and an insistence on the purity of rude health. Here the poor clerk found it difficult to meet conflicting demands, isolated and criticised by life-style and etiquette guides for his weakness in body and mind and tendency to indolence, yet encouraged in pursuits that seemed to prioritise an onanistic attention to the physical self. Thus the author of *The Commercial Clerk and his Success* bemoaned that:

> There has unfortunately sprung up in the past decade a certain section of young clerks who call themselves keen sportsmen, but yet who have hardly played and whose capacities for sport consist in their ability to cram into their heads a host of statistics concerning professional players.

and then proceeded to advocate extreme antidotes:

> an inexpensive and efficacious stimulant is for the young man to strip on rising and vigorously rub himself down for five minutes with a rough towel after sponging the body with tepid water. There are many young men who are physically unable to take a cold bath, but none are too delicate to indulge in this health producing practice.[20]

Complementing this, popular definitions of the clerk type compared his pale spare frame unfavourably with that other icon of the Victorian city street, the navvy. The novelist H. Greaves usefully employed sartorial codes to make the distinctions explicit:

> It was in Fenchurch Street. He had stopped for a moment to watch a knot of workmen repair the roadway – the pleasant ring of the swinging hammers exercising quite a fascination over the little crowd of city men and youths standing on the pavement, looking as though they would like to step out from beneath their silk hats and from out of their frock coats, and forget the sordid grind of office work in a healthy exercise of the hands with those same sledgehammers.[21]

However, despite attempts to isolate the clerk as an example of physical and moral weakness, office culture paradoxically offered its own model of homosocial exclusivity within which body and clothing formed both a bonding badge and an important marker of position in a highly stratified professional atmosphere. Fashionability in the usual sense did not necessarily dictate modes of dressing, though competition obviously fuelled a desire to consume in some cases (figure 17). The opening line of *The Brass Ring – The Extraordinary Adventures of a City Clerk*, an adventure story published in 1904, clearly communicated the importance of distinctions which were encouraged by the politics of the workplace:

> William Lester Craik was engaged at the office of a city stockbroker. His

17 A group of young middle-class males in formal day wear, *c.* 1885, studio of McGregor, photographer. Kilmarnock, Scotland. Prosperity and respectability are the social attributes suggested by the neat, well-cut suits of the men pictured here. Beyond the surface uniformity, however, each ensemble shows subtle marks of distinction in texture, pattern and trimming. Far from renouncing the will to display, these sitters have orchestrated highly individualised variations of an adaptable theme

chief ambitions were to be dressed more stylishly than anyone in his office, and (with a view to higher things in the neighbourhood of Throgmorton Street) to earn a reputation for shrewdness and punctuality.[22]

Just as usual though, in similar representations of working life were those descriptions betraying an attention to minute differentiation in dress or the mundane detail of the office environment, which served to prioritise the repetitive and repressive structures of a nine-to-five existence, giving meaning to social processes and relationships which were generally perceived as being meaningless. The novelist Shan Bullock, writing as his alter-ego Robert Thorne in the autobiographical *Story of a London Clerk* of 1907 illuminated such precise office rituals, as rich in their way as the narratives of dressing and undressing which pre-occupied the writers of women's magazines. Here the routine evening departure of an elderly colleague becomes a litany evoking the careful orchestration of time and the negotiation of peculiarly masculine commodities, familiar to the clerk throughout his career:

> Into drawers he cleared his table, each pencil daintily lifted and deposited, the paper knife in its appointed place, the scissors in its own corner, and so on till everything was stowed and locked away. Then he washed carefully; brushed his hair and whiskers, emptied the pockets of his office clothes upon the table; changed behind a screen; folded his office clothes; put watch away and tapped the outside of its pocket to make sure that it was there, put keys in this trouser pocket and tapped them, money in that pocket and tapped it, handkerchief in another and tapped it; at last, when gold pencil and toothpick, snuff box and card case all were put away and tapped, he tried his drawers, tapped himself all over again, put on silk hat and overcoat, took his umbrella from the stand, wished us good day and went.[23]

This concurrent rejection and celebration of a tangible masculine corporeality is perhaps best epitomised in a pamphlet of 1877 entitled *Manliness* and delivered to the Victoria Street Church Young Men's Literary Society, Derby, which made the tensions between manliness as controlled surface and sensual forbearance explicit:

> Manliness is not an affair of patent leather boots, or of tight fitting kid gloves, or of exquisite beard and moustache ... Conventionalism is not manliness, foppery is not manliness ... Manly character is the grandest thing beneath the stars, and the day will dawn upon this sorely confused world of ours when the highest places will be filled by men, and the only nobility will be the nobility of manly character ... It is the thing of greatest worth in God's sight. It is the temple in which he dwells.[24]

'Sorely confused' is perhaps an apposite description of the late twentieth-century fashion historian's reaction to the multiplicity of meanings inherent in official and popular constructions of late nineteenth-century masculinities. It also describes the condition of the Victorian menswear retailer and consumer, faced with models of ideal manhood that condemned conventionalism and foppery on equal terms, and demands an examination of more oppositional popular masculine forms that must have offered alternatives to the status quo. To focus further on that rich and largely untapped seam of commentary surrounding respectable working- and lower-middle-class culture (untapped that is by historians of clothing), it has been well established by historians of popular culture that between 1850 and 1930 the comics and artistes of the music hall, alongside anti-heroical descriptions of Hooligan gangs in the popular press, provided a loud-checked, bowler-hatted and bewhiskered icon of self-satisfied, belligerent masculinity for the 'masher' or young man around town (figure 18);

18 Two young men, *c.*1900, provenance unknown (British postcard). The cult of the 'masher' allowed young urban men remarkable potential for interpreting fashionable masculine style and often subverting it. Here, short, tight trousers, ostentatious watch chains, bowler hats and patterned ties make a mockery of conservative suburban values

19 Music hall swells, *c.*1895, provenance unknown. The music hall repertoire embraced a wide range of acts that drew their humour and topicality from the absurdities of contemporary dress and social behaviour. The aristocratic swell played a prominent role on the stage between 1860 and 1914, his drunken ostentatious patter and flaunting of luxurious evening dress serving both as class satire and a fashionable role model

theatrical confections that tally well with G. A. Sala's journalistic observations of 'spruce young clerks' radiant on the pavements of Fleet Street and The Strand in the late 1850s:

> dashing young parties who purchase the pea green, the orange and the rose pink gloves; the crimson braces, the kaleidoscopic shirt studs, the shirts embroidered with dahlias, deaths heads, race horses, sunflowers and ballet girls.[25]

Alongside the brash vulgarity of the masher, the neatly trimmed, tightly suited and primly booted bon viveur offered a more aspirational model of 'swelldom' to the rising sons of newly affluent suburban districts, satirised most memorably by the figure of Lupin in Grossmith's *Diary of a Nobody*; suggested by H. G. Wells's upwardly mobile shop-boy *Kipps* who, stirred by 'grave discussions about collars, ties and the proper shape of a boot toe ... purchased ... three stand up collars that left a red mark under his ears';[26] and also evoked again by Robert Thorne, where the author reminisces about his early days in the tax office at Somerset House:

> I can see myself now, stalking home with shoulders raised and elbows crooked, less a parody of the lordly than of the storks in Kew Gardens. I bought a cane, a misfit tailed coat, a cheap silk hat, an assortment of neckties and high collars. I had my pipe and cigarette case … Young my friends, very young.[27]

Further afield, a description of a Cardiff shop assistant, published in the *Cardiff Times* of 1886 conveys the currency that metropolitan models held in the provinces:

> Our friend wears a Newmarket coat. In his hand he carries a ponderous walking stick, and when he meets a friend, he salutes him with a sentence from the latest melodrama. He transforms his bedroom into a miniature theatre, the walls of which are profusely decorated with the illustrated advertisements of dramatic companies.[28]

Social historian Peter Bailey, in his suggestive study of the music-hall swell song, describes the precise but multiple visual attractions that stage figures like George Leybourne's 'Champagne Charlie' conveyed to audiences made up of such characters from the late 1860s onwards (figure 19). On the one hand, the appearance of the performer, often verged on caricature:

> The stage swell paraded all the apparatus of genteel apparel, though variation and distortion were common where the object was parody. Thus Arthur Lloyd often performed in bizarre dress and make up, sporting a coat with exaggerated lapels, an outlandish silk choker and a forty Cardigan power moustache.[29]

While on the other hand, contemporary accounts such as Percy Fitzgerald's *Music Hall Land* of 1890 recorded the tendency of variety regulars to model their apparel on precisely those figures and trends lampooned on stage:

> The quiet airy reserve and nonchalance of the stage gentleman would seem at the music hall to be unintelligible, or uninteresting. But the East-ender has created his idea from a gentleman or 'gent' of which he has had glimpses at the bars and finds it in perfection at his music hall. At the music hall, everything is tinselled over; and we find a kind of racy gin-born affectation to be the mode, everyone being 'dear boy' or a 'pal' … There is a suggestion of perpetual dress suit, with deep side pockets, in which the hands are ever plunged; indeed a true gentleman will rather hire his suit for the occasion – always costly and involving a deposit – rather than fail in these conveniences. And we must ever recollect to strut and stride rather than walk.[30]

Bailey suggests that the very physicality of music-hall spectacle, combined with the emulative appeal of many of the songs, in itself encouraged an attention to sartorial presentation among the predominantly male audience:

> The music hall was in one respect quite literally the mirror of fashion. From its early days the music hall had made extensive use of mirror glass, a feature inherited from the gin palace. As well as providing a greater illusion of space and comfort, the mirrors made for an increased self consciousness of bearing and appearance. 'All round the hall', remarked a review of the refurbished Middlesex in 1872, 'handsome mirrors reflect the glittering lights, and offer abundant opportunities for self admiration.' As the lion comique paraded his fashionable self on stage, members of his audience could with a sidelong glance decide how their image matched up to that of their hero.[31]

It is perhaps no coincidence that these are physical descriptions reminiscent of contemporary representations of department store ambience in their emphasis on qualities of luxury, display and narcissistic absorption, more usually identified with spaces for female as opposed to male consumption, but increasingly associated with the publicity attached to the renovation and refitting of many tailoring shops and men's departments after the turn of the century. Such suggestive evidence shows how it is possible to begin to prise a notion of self-conscious, popular, masculine fashionability from the dress codes and architecture of elements of organised, indeed commodified working- and lower-middle-class urban culture. This is not to suggest an all-embracing celebration of sartorial excess; signs of a more familiar uniformity clearly interweave with differing levels of self-awareness and denial. In the figure of Robert Thorne, Shan Bullock presented perhaps a more typical image of the alienated, modern city drone that offers an oppressive contrast to the exuberance of the music-hall turn:

> Can I find heart to scoff at that figure I see in his bowler hat and long overcoat, stepping valiantly to work through all the hazards of London winter weather. His hands are deep in his pockets, his collar high about the ears. The rim of his hat is carefully inked in the places worn by much brushing; his overcoat shows a hint of green about the shoulders, the bottoms of his trousers are fraying, his boots have metal protectors upon the heels ... There are thousands like him. There they go hurrying for the bridges, each in his cheap black coat, each with pale face and uneven shoulders ... Slaves of the desk. Two-penny clerks.[32]

So, as the surviving descriptions and representations suggest, the respectable male consumer undoubtedly faced a problematic public discourse of fashionable masculinity which, while focusing on the external healthiness and physical glory of the male body, demanded a rigorous attention to structures of self denial and social distinction, difficult to maintain in an arena of expanded consumer choice. By 1900 advances in manufacturing systems and retailing techniques offered a growing market the prospect of increasingly sophisticated ready-made suits alongside a continuing emphasis on British bespoke tailoring. A wide range of subtly varying styles was available for consumption with an almost fetishistic attention to detail and differentiation in terms of trimming, texture, colour and cut; and a finish indicative of modernity, suggesting the existence of a carefully honed, highly detailed sartorial rhetoric around which men were able to construct individual, yet conventional identities, adapted for the office, workshop, sports field, theatre and sea front. The menswear retailer H. Dennis Bradley presented a typically rigid, though self-consciously modern guide for fashionable dressing in his catalogue for the Bond Street tailoring firm Pope and Bradley in 1912:

> Worn alike by all classes, the necessity of having one's lounge suits well cut is obvious. The subtle details which elevate the expert cutter to a plane above the lesser lights of his profession are never more pronounced than in this important garment ... For Town wear it is always advisable to have a fairly well-shaped coat with the waistline defined without being in anyway accentuated. Tweeds for country and knockabout wear should have a more negligée effect. Any extreme fashion is entirely out of keeping with the character and term of a 'lounge'.[33]

It may not be too far-fetched to suggest that such promotional constructions traverse barriers of work and pleasure to incorporate a gendered appreciation of the qualities of tailoring; echoing those areas of leisured cultural activity such as collecting, prioritised for men in the guise of connoiseurship while being demoted for women to the realm of the domestic chore or the trivial hobby. A hidden language of clothing demanding the 'connoisseur's eye' may have released male fashion from accusations of effeminacy in a similar manner, and a closer examination of its grammar and meaning would certainly allow for a more searching and innovative investigation of the status of male clothing as a socially constructed 'object', producing shared meaning between men, than the culturally simplistic explanations offered by the traditional dress history acceptance of a pervasive denial. If anything, rather than signifying the much-quoted 'great masculine renunciation', or male rejection of style change and sartorial expression, the self-denying rhetoric of tailoring journals and etiquette manuals, and its reflection in novels and on the stage actually reveals a rigorous attention to the rules and details of dress which in itself constitutes an alternative fashion system.

Nevertheless, despite evidence of carefully calibrated guidelines and opportunities for self-expression, fashion history leaves us with an image of unrelenting conformity that sits well with nineteenth- and early twentieth-century interpretations of respectable manliness, but leads no further in unpacking the contents of, or alternatives to, a seeming undifferentiation in dress. Once isolated from this interpretative straitjacket, I hope to have shown that a figure as seemingly mundane and ubiquitous as the clerk, can suggest both a thriving, though problematised engagement with notions of a mainstream masculine fashionability and a more theatrical sense of escapism; while the resounding silences and denouncements proffered by trade publications, popular literature and moralising pamphlets directed towards his kind, in themselves speak of a vigorously contested arena of sartorial choice. It is hoped that future research in the history of menswear, in adopting a more sophisticated reading of representational material, combined with a wider investigation of the material context of menswear production and retailing, will help to flesh out the aspirations, tastes and opinions of those men who, against the odds of all those received notions concerning the place of masculinity within consumer culture and a family based economy, in a strange reflection of the attitudes embraced by Wilde, might have agreed with the proposal of that pin-up of the clerk class, Marie Lloyd, that 'a little of what you fancy does you good'.

Notes

1 R. Felski, *The Gender of Modernity*, Cambridge, Mass., Harvard University Press, 1995; M. Boscagli, *Eye on the Flesh: Fashions of Masculinity in the Early Twentieth Century*, Oxford, Westview Press, 1996; R. Gagnier, *Idylls of the Marketplace: Oscar Wilde and the Victorian Public*, Aldershot, Scolar Press, 1986.

2 J. C. Flügel, *The Psychology of Clothes*, London, Hogarth Press, 1966.

3 A. Adburgham, *Shops and Shopping 1800–1914*, London, Allen & Unwin, 1981, pp. 137–48.

4 S. Levitt, *Victorians Unbuttoned*, London, Allen & Unwin, 1986.

5 G. McCracken, *Culture and Consumption*, Indianapolis, Indiana University Press, 1990; C. Campbell, *The Romantic Ethic and the Spirit of Modern Consumerism*, Oxford, Blackwell, 1987.

6 R. Williams, *Dream Worlds: Mass Consumption in Late Nineteenth-Century France*, Los Angeles, University of California Press, 1982.

7 F. W. Burgess, *The Practical Retail Draper: A Complete Guide for the Drapery and Allied Trades*, London, Virtue & Co., 1912.

8 L. Davidoff, and C. Hall, *Family Fortunes: Men and Women of the English Middle Class 1780–1850*, London, Routledge, 1987.

9 R. Bowlby, *Just Looking: Consumer Culture in Dreisser, Gissing and Zola*, London, Methuen, 1985.

10 N. Cott, 'On Men's History and Women's History' in M. C. Carnes and C. Griffen (eds), *Meanings for Manhood: Constructions of Masculinity in Victorian America*, Chicago, University of Chicago Press, 1990, p. 207.

11 S. Pearson, *Weekday Living: A Book for Young Men and Women*, London, Kegan, Paul, Trench, 1882.

12 Pearson, *Weekday Living*.

13 H. Greaves, *The Commercial Clerk and his Success*, London, Cassell, 1909.

14 Anon, *The Story of A London Clerk: A Faithful Narrative, Faithfully Told*, London, Leadenhall Press, 1896.

15 E. Pugh, *The City of the World: A Book about London and the Londoner*, London, Thomas Nelson, 1908.

16 M. Fall, *London Town: Sketches of Life and Character*, London, Tinsley Bros, 1896.

17 A. Mangan and J. Walvin, *Manliness and Morality: Middle-Class Masculinity in Britain and America 1800–1940*, Manchester, Manchester University Press, 1987.

18 *Publicity: A Practical Guide for the Retail Clothier and Outfitter*, London, The Outfitter, 1910, p. 38.

19 R. Dellamora, 'Homosexual Scandal and Compulsory Heterosexuality in the 1890s', in L. Pyckett (ed.), *Reading Fin de Siècle Fictions*, London, Longman, 1996.

20 Greaves, *The Commercial Clerk*.

21 Anon, *The Story of A London Clerk*.

22 E. Downey, *The Brass Ring: The Extraordinary Adventures of a City Clerk*, London, 1904, p. 1.

23 S. Bullock, *Robert Thorne: The Story of a London Clerk*, London: Werner Laurie, 1907, p. 141.

24 W. Crosby, *Manliness: An Address delivered to the Victoria Street Church Young Men's Literary Society, Derby*, London, Hodder & Stoughton, 1877, p. 4.

25 G. A. Sala, *Twice Round the Clock, or the Hours of the Day in London*, London, 1859.

26 H. G. Wells, *Kipps*, London, Everyman, 1993, p. 37.

27 Bullock, *Robert Thorne*.

28 *Cardiff Times*, 'Behind the Counter: Sketches by a Shop Assistant', Aberdare, George Jones, 1886, p. 8.

29 P. Bailey, 'Champagne Charlie: Performance and Ideology in the Music Hall Swell Song', in J. S. Bratton (ed.), *Music Hall: Performance and Style*, Milton Keynes, Open University Press, 1986, p. 59.

30 P. Fitzgerald, *Music Hall Land*, London, Ward & Downey, 1890, p. 4.

31 Bailey, 'Champagne Charlie', p. 61.

32 Bullock, *Robert Thorne*.

33 H. D. Bradley, *Vogue*, London, 1912, p. 22.

5 ✧ That little magic touch: the headtie

Carol Tulloch

T HE 'image and language of the clothed body' has been credited with wielding enormous social influence. The inanimate objects employed to create the clothed body are physically destitute of life, yet clothes have the conflicting ability to initiate and confirm change, to broadcast the political conflict or status within a community; and to be a metaphor of domination and conversely opposition.[1] Accessories should not be forgotten as part of this definition. They are the 'little magic touch' deployed by professional and amateur stylists to perfect a desired look. Generally it is the body, that is, the torso, that is primed as the place of action for the clothed body.[2] Accessories which dress the head, hands and feet can, in their own right, supply a cultural and social narrative.[3]

The focus for this chapter is the relationship between young Black British women of Jamaican descent and the self-assembly headtie they wore during the 1970s. The study considers how this relationship was simultaneously affected by Black British women's social values and cultural identity, which was shaped by their existence in Britain, and the transnational influence of African–Americans. I wish to argue that as part of their feminist discourse, Black British women used the headtie to identify themselves as 'Womanist',[4] to be seen and taken seriously. African–American author Alice Walker proclaims a 'Womanist' to be: 'A black feminist or feminist of colour'; a woman who has moved away from 'girlish' things into the heady responsibility of womanhood; a Black woman thirsty for knowledge, a black woman who wants to take control of her life and is purposeful and steadfast in this pursuit. But Walker maintains that it can also refer to all women regardless of race and sexual orientation. This apolitical slant on the term has caused consternation among black feminists in America and Britain.[5] This chapter proposes that Black British women employed the term womanist as part of their engagement in cultural and political debates through the affective application of their clothed bodies. Furthermore, it proposes that the headtie, as part of black British women's search for a new, expressive cultural identity in the 1970s, consciously tied them closer to the cultural aesthetic of African–America and Jamaica, formidable players in the development of an African diaspora aesthetic.

The 1970s was a momentous period in the development of the African diaspora and black identity, when the cumulative activities of the civil rights, Black Power and black-consciousness movements had a crucial influence. African–Americans looked at their segregated world with new eyes. In 1968 they were encouraged by black activists and musicians to 'Think Black, Talk Black, Create Black, Buy Black, Vote Black and Live Black'.[6] Thus the African–American community aimed to take control of and impose their own cultural disunion, as a people who were all too well aware of the crippling emotional, social and economic effects of the official American segregation laws. This reversed, self-imposed form of segregation came at a time when the segregation laws were being dissolved. It was a strong, deliberate backlash designed to create a solid counter cultural identity based on being 'black', which at the time was translated to mean of African origin, not a displaced, invisible 'negro'. This resulted in an electrical charge of creativity on all cultural levels for the community, not least through dress and self-image.

The black streetstyles which sprang from this situation identified African–Americans around the western world as possessing perhaps the highest level of street credibility in terms of dress, music and language. During the late 1950s, the commitment of 'Black Bohemia'[7] to the black freedom movement and African liberation, and the subsequent early stages of black pride in the early 1960s, African–American youths appeared to lead the way in asserting 'blackness':

> 'Black' was viewed by many older, more conservative African-Americans with confusion, suspicion, and amusement, the younger and more outspoken members of the race saw the change as not only symbolic, but an emphatic proclamation of an oppressed people's psychological reorientation.[8]

The 1970s witnessed the high point of anti-fashion as a political statement. Valerie Steele claims it covertly diffused the political radicalism engaged by a series of movements across Europe and America in the 1960s, to reach the masses in the 1970s. Steele suggests the 1970s produced two periods of anti-fashion activity. The first phase, what she terms as a mix of 'late hippie diffusion' left over from the late 1960s, lasted from 1970–74 and included a distinctive African–American style of dress of African influences such as the African dashiki, as worn by the 'Black Moses', African–American soul artist Isaac Hayes; a penchant for urban guerrilla dress of leather immortalised by the Black Power movement, and the pimp-inspired, ostentatious, eye-popping style of platforms and gargantuan flares, and body-hugging polo-neck sweaters epitomised by the likes of black screen god, Shaft.[9] The second phase of 1975–79 was shaped by the ambiguous presence of the highly aggressive dress of punk and the exacting conservatism of 'Dress-for-Success uniformity'.[10] The headcloths worn by African–Americans during the 1970s, Steele suggests, were employed partly due to their strong links with Africa as 'a more overtly politicized version of the wider interests in "ethnic" style'.[11]

This distinctive form of African–American radical chic was the antithesis of the image presented in mainstream films featuring African–American women up to 1970, and, through skin-colour association, extended to all black women of the African diaspora. Hollywood perpetuated a demeaning image of black womanhood. Throughout the gradual, global domination of the American film industry at the beginning of this century, the predominant roles Hollywood offered African–American actresses were the three (often combined) low-status characters: slave, servant or 'Mammy'.[12] Stephen Bourne recounts how the latter category stereotyped black women as 'a passive, one-dimensional, comical, non-threatening, docile caricature of black womanhood'.[13] For Bourne, in spite of this stereotype, the appearance of African–American actress Hattie McDaniel in seventy-odd screen portrayals of the Mammy was imbued with depth, intelligence, wit and sass, a combination immortalised in the 1939 Hollywood blockbuster *Gone With The Wind*. In her myriad roles as Mammy, McDaniel wore a variety of headtie designs from the clinical, neatly trussed style of *Gone With The Wind* where a small piece of fabric is secured closely to the head, and the ends are tied, rolled upwards and tucked in tightly at the front, to the exuberant style with a floppy knot at the front of the head, generally associated with the caricatured image of the Mammy, as worn by McDaniel in *Show Boat*.

Intensive distaste for these representations of black womanhood was high among the African–American community. During the Second World War, African–American servicemen claimed McDaniel's screen image in *Gone With The Wind* lowered their morale.[14] The irony was that on the home front the style of headtie featured in the film had acquired a high fashion status among Caucasian munitions workers and civilians committed to the war effort in both America and Britain. It was worn as protective headwear, as well as a fashion feature and became a signifier of patriotic fervour. The stereotyped screen attire and image of African–American female characters during the first fifty years or so of American cinema belied their off-screen image of high-fashion sophistication and modernity as exemplified by such icons as the Jazz artist Billie Holiday. Black women, then, were represented as a homogeneous entity, devoid of an individual identity, devalued and servile. In this context the headtie signified the delineation of a perennial inferiority.

In 1972 African–American artist Betye Sarr's composition 'The Liberation of Aunt Jemima' attempted to salvage the Mammy image. It features a large figurine of a black woman in complete Mammy regalia: bowed headtie, a bandanna around her neck, a rifle in one hand, a broom in the other. In front of this figure is a framed picture of another Mammy. She has one hand on her hips, and a white baby under her other arm. Behind the figurine is a Warholesque head repeat of a 'grinning' black woman, her only form of decoration is a headband. The work is an effective *memoria technica* of black female existence and opposition in the face of adversity.

Since the 1970s, Black British women have also fashioned themselves to produce aesthetic identities based on the fusion of their own experiences as members of a black counter-culture which operates within the white hegemony of Britain, with all the political and cultural complexities this combination entails. These women were part of a historically significant group, first-generation, postwar black people born in Britain due to the great number of Caribbean and African men, women and children who emigrated to Britain between 1948 and 1962, as a result of England's positive immigration policy. The parents of these young men and women came from predominantly black populated countries that had maintained their specific form of Caribbean or African culture. The diaspora experience of, for example, Jamaican parents and their British-born children was, inevitably, different and frequently difficult. None the less during the black-consciousness fervour of the 1970s, the diaspora identities created by Black British women as part of a feminist-cultural discourse was based on, and celebrated, the diaspora experience, which resulted in a 'diaspora aesthetic' that drew on ideas and 'traditions' that developed during slavery, and were reconfigured continuously. Stuart Hall has argued that the diaspora experience

> is defined not by essence or purity, but by the recognition of a necessary heterogeneity and diversity; by a conception of 'identity' which lives with and through, not despite, difference; by hybridity. Diaspora identities are those which are constantly producing and reproducing themselves anew, through transformation and difference.[15]

The tie that binds

I have chosen to focus on the headtie as it is one of the few pieces of apparel worn by black women throughout the African diaspora that can be traced back to their African cultural heritage from the mid-eighteenth century, and has been in use continuously through to the present.[16] The headtie enabled African-born slave women and their descendants through-out the diaspora to maintain links with their African cultural heritage.[17] The use of the headtie in public by Black British women from the 1970s onwards has a particular resonance. Whether worn as a tower of fabric bound tight around the head, a folded square or a triangle of cloth tied tight to the head and secured at the back, front or side in a neat knot, or in the luxurious style of a length of fabric wrapped around the head, the ends left free to cascade down onto the body, the headtie enabled Black British women to engage in a public embrace with African–American, Caribbean and African women, and symbolised the ambitions and potency of the term pan-African.

The head-covering is known by a variety of names as: 'turban'; 'head-wrap'; 'bandanna'; 'headrag'; 'head handkerchief'; 'tie head' and 'headtie'. I find the latter is the most appropriate to consolidate the historical bond between the accessory and the wearer in America and Jamaica, and its use by Black British women of Jamaican descent during the 1970s. Patricia Hunt's study of the American towns of Georgia and South Carolina shows that they had a large concentration of slaves who were central to the production of cotton prior to and following the American Civil War. The headtie was worn by black women at both junctures. There was a lifecycle of cotton from seed to plant, and from fibre to cloth, which in turn supplied slave women with 'headwraps'.[18] This process exemplified the lack of distinction between the use of the cotton cloth by female slave plantation workers and their intrinsic role in the production process of cotton for human consumption. This symbiosis intensified the invisible position of female (and male) slaves, as their true identity had been suppressed by the plantation/slave owner through the removal of their language, their traditions and their original family name.

I would suggest that the headtie symbolised the tie between the slave and the production of cotton on the plantation. It also was a metaphor for the inextricable tie between the plantation owner and the slave owner. Furthermore it was an allegory for the volatile and transient tie between master and slave. These relationships were not exclusive to America as, for example, slaves in Jamaica endured the same form of controlled tie.[19] Within this historical context the headtie acted as presage.

In Jamaica the headtie was omnipresent during the late-nineteenth and early-twentieth centuries. This was a period of extensive reconstruction and modernisation following emancipation in 1834 and the Morant Bay Re-bellion in 1865 which preceded the formation of a Crown Colony government. The British colony was dominated by four main ethnic groups: African–Jamaicans, white Jamaicans, mixed race and Indians. The market trader or higgler, domestic servants and agricultural workers, all claimed the headtie as a central feature of their regalia. In the case of the higgler, the headtie provided extra padding along with the cotta to support goods they transported on their heads. Agricultural labour was dirty and arduous,

20 Jamaica 1903. This postcard depicts a washer-woman who is representative of the African–Jamaican female working class. Despite the servile pose, her personal image is clean and simple with the prominent accent of decoration directed at the chequered headtie

21 Early 1880s. The fashionably elegant image of the young woman centre left, in the slender style of the princess-line dress, is counterbalanced by her voluminous headtie. The evocative ensemble pushes the headtie into the realm of leisure dress

22 Jamaica *c.* 1900. These structured headties could be described as toques, which accentuate the clean line of the women's dress

23 Jamaica 1903. This market trader wears a headtie similar to the madras handkerchief check. The ostentatious use of the fabric indicates that the whole handkerchief, a metre square, was used

and for them the headtie was a necessary protective item. British and American travel writers promoted African–Jamaican working class women as a homogeneous entity. They concentrated on the functional detail and styling techniques to categorise the dress style of a class and race: the black peasantry. The group was dissected further by the writers. They categorised 'the bright bandanna women' [20] or the higglers, as a subculture. Travel writer Mabel Blanche Caffin likened the peasantry to the London cockneys in their misuse of the English language, a comparison that drew cultural similarities in the dress of the Jamaican higgler and the cockney coster-mongers. These subcultures linked through Empire compiled a uniform that focused on accessories and styling (for example, in London golf cap, popularly known as the flat-cloth cap became a coster badge of com-munity). This example demonstrates how an attention to detail and styling by men and women made such features into characteristic symbols of their respective counter-cultures. In Jamaica, Caffin was so taken with the headtie that she suggested them as potential souvenirs to the plutocratic tourists for whom she wrote, an example of a nineteenth-century subcultural item being adopted by members of the dominant culture.

24 Kingston, Jamaica 1894. The headties of the respectably dressed domestic ser-vants are indicative of their lower and higher positions within the service. The meagre shapes equate with simple dress and the elaborate constructions equate with elaborate bodices

25 Jamaica 1891–94. There is no indication whether these Indian women are immigrants or Jamaican–Indians. What is evident is their race as Indian. Their use of the madras check headtie in tandem with Western dress in the British colony of Jamaica amplifies these women as 'Other'

In reality the headtie was worn by African–Jamaican and Indian women as part of both occupational and fine dress. It appears, from photographic evidence that this self-constructed accessory was socially acceptable among the working-class black community at weddings, church meetings or for market day. From the 1880s onwards, a series of headtie shapes emerged that invites the consideration of style trends. These included a closely bound, unstructured style, a forerunner of the late twentieth-century small 'bandanna' headtie, the ends tied at the back towards the nape of the neck, which provided an even surface to transport goods; a turbanesque shape, loosely bound with ties brought round to the front of the head and knotted towards the crown, making use of a large expanse of fabric, appears to have been reserved for leisure; a structured design incorporating sharp folds and creases to frame the head, which sits like a hat, revealing the ears, and secured by knotting the ends together high above the back of the neck; and a plain flat-fronted headtie with a burst of fabric at the nape of the neck, making full use of the 'handkerchief', a square metre of woven fabric (see figures 20–3). A wide variety of cloths of multifarious designs were used. The majority of the headties were formed from the south Indian real madras handkerchief.[21] The history of the fabric has

26 Britain mid-late 1970s. The dancers relate to their unity in their cultural and racial roots through dress and dance. Significantly, the chosen style of headtie bears close resemblance to that worn by the fashion-conscious African–Jamaican woman ninety years earlier (figure 21)

particular resonance to the relationship between the Indian and Jamaican peasantry during the period. Prior to the abolition of the slave trade in 1808,[22] the real madras handkerchief was a currency of slavery, associated with the 'triangle of trade'. It was manufactured in southern Indian villages, then transported to London to be auctioned to either the Royal Africa Company or private traders, and finally the cloth was used to barter for slaves in West Africa and to clothe slaves in the West Indies. This system of trading continued following abolition. The real madras handkerchief, now defined as a 'prohibited good' by Britain, benefited from the practice of rescinding duties on re-exports from London. The West Indies remained one of the markets where the cloth was sold alongside the British-produced imitation madras handkerchiefs.[23]

Despite variations, the generic style of the headtie established a group identity. The black peasantry were bound together in the adoption of an accessory, and more specifically in the use of the real madras handkerchief whose history dates back to the slavery period.[24] It is impressive that this apparently humble object can possess such a complex historical story and broad cultural influence. The headtie symbolised the tie between African–Jamaican women, and the emergent tie between African–Jamaican women and Indian women as 'Other', despite the vast cultural and linguistic gulf that divided them (figure 25). In the headtie itself, there had also developed a relationship 'between masses, areas, forms, lines and colours'.[25] In its longevity the headtie acquired an aura of simplicity that embodied a community relationship based on shared historical roots, colonialism and difference.

A decade in the life of . . .

Patrizia Calefato has deconstructed the close relationship between clothes, dress, fashion and style, and placed fashion as the medium which

> turned the body into a discourse, a sign, a thing ... A body permeated by discourse, of which clothes and objects are an intrinsic part, is a body exposed to transformations, ... a body that will feel and taste all that the world feels and tastes, if it simply lets itself open up.[26]

Alternatively, clothing forms the material components of dress, the intrinsic tools which 'exposes the body to a limitless metamorphosis'.[27] Catherine King's reading of the three-dimensional clothed body, and the very act of dressing, adorning and styling is 'the skilled production of more or less lasting objects and visual images', that equates with 'art-making'.[28] Style, on the other hand, edits the flimflam of the various, and sometimes confused, messages transmitted through fashion, and cuts to the chase of the central point of subjective identities being visually discussed between clothed bodies. The biography of things – objects and the clothed body – at a particular time and space can reveal the identity of the users and 'make salient what might otherwise remain obscure.'[29] Igor Kopytoff has argued that people and objects are both constructed by society and the social world they inhabit, and are therefore not separate – objects as commodities and people as individuation. The social patterns and structures of 'complex societies' are the same as those which affect the commodities produced and used in such societies and thereby perpetrate the 'uncertainty of identity'. In such a situation there is leverage for dynamic interaction between the inanimate and animated.[30] This ability of the body to change with the application of clothing in a structured, premeditated way, as surmised by Calefato, is fraught with hidden meanings and questions. What is the identity of the clothed body in relation to the clothing and styling it adopts, and does it bear any relation to the wearer's real cultural identity? The course of cultural-identity formulation, within any culture, is not a smooth progression. In the case of young Black British women, the process is profound and compounded by the didactic power of British hegemony, the media, current trends and peer pressure – from black and white people – to conform to the 'established' cultural norm. My own experience of, and reasons for, wearing the headtie during the 1970s, acts as a microscopic insight into the experiences faced by black British women to excavate a cultural identity. By drawing on specific points of an identified relationship with an object, and within the wider context of their combined social relationship, an 'autobiography' of their relationship can present some semblance of a 'collective address'.[31]

I was born in Doncaster, South Yorkshire, of Jamaican parents who immigrated to Britain in the mid-1950s. Between the age of five and sixteen I lived a dual existence. My public and private worlds were shaped and kept separate by two different cultures: British society in the public sphere, and a Jamaican creole culture alongside the images and influences from television, the radio, newspapers and magazines infused my private world. Only sporadically did the Jamaican culture inform the British influences. The dress and hairstyles of my early teens were influenced by these two worlds. In the main I wore the latest European-inspired fashion trends. I processed my hair, a method of 'controlling' black hair, which was a vain (in both senses of the word) attempt to keep in line with European hairstyles. Like many of my black and white peers, I eventually flirted with subcultural, that is, white, subcultural dress. My identity was essentially that of a 'coloured' girl in European guise. In the home, I would often wear a headtie, like my mother and grandmother had always done while housekeeping or as part of our laborious hairdressing techniques. The headtie was either worn tied close to the head and secured with a small knot at the nape of the neck, or the ends brought round to the front and tied very tightly, or the mammy style, with a large bow, but this was frowned upon by my mother. This style signified for her too much of the 'negro', too much servility, as depicted in the Sunday afternoon films we watched as a family between morning and evening church service. To the older generation, the 'black headtie' was a utilitarian garment to be worn only in the home, as a form of 'undress'. In public, my mother and grandmother wore the respectable establishment headscarf as worn by Queen Elizabeth II and their fellow working-class white neighbours and workmates. The silk or acetate square was folded and secured onto the head by tying the triangle under the chin. Within working-class traditions, the style has been worn by Whitby fisher women as documented in the evocative nineteenth-century photographs of Frank Meadow Sutcliffe, European peasantry and char women of the post-Second World War period, but also became a universal style adopted in particular by upper-class country women from the 1930s onwards.

From my mid-teenage years onwards, the mood shifted gear dramatically. Black culture, specifically the diaspora cultures of Africa, America and Jamaica, infiltrated both my public and private worlds, in what appears to have been an instant. Black music – soul, funk and reggae – and musicians, 'Blaxploitation' films and actors, political activists such as the black radical icon of the 1960s, Angela Davis, who had not lost her potency in 1970s Britain, the emergent Rastafarians and sports personalities were in abundance and visible in all forms of the media. I no longer wanted the European look. I wanted to copy Aretha Franklin and the Jackson Five, the *Superfly* film characters Cleopatra Jones and Shaft. On visits to what I believed to be Britain's black utopia, Brixton, a district in the city of London, I jealously admired the young black women I saw on the streets. They appeared to me as enlightened, majestic women, light years ahead of me in terms of style and black-consciousness. I wanted the Afro and Afro-puffs hairstyle. Most poignantly, I wanted the elaborately styled headties I saw worn with pride on the streets by black women, or by the black celebrities I watched on television. The headtie had been liberated, it was no longer hidden from the world of street dress but had become an essential glamour item, using swathes of fabric to create a variety of styles that towered upwards, or wrapped close to the head with long trains left free to cascade down the wearer's neck and body. These eloquent designs resonated with the new-found confidence felt by black women throughout the diaspora, during this time of cultural awakening: they now had the strength in numbers to rely on and expose their 'blackness'; they acquired the confidence to draw from their history for inspiration. Conversely, the Mammy style was prohibited from encroaching on public space as it was, in the minds of black women, imbued with the painful memories of servitude and degradation endured by black women (and men) from slavery to the middle of the twentieth century.

In the 1970s, the headtie expanded the repertoire of style images available to black women. Its fashionability during this explosive period of black expression in Britain swept through the generational ranks of Britain's black counter-culture; grandmothers and mothers joined their daughters and adopted the style in public, thus reducing the age gap, and thereby achieved a level of 'Oneness' through the use of a particular apparel. Through an exuberant, politically charged act of visual arbitration over the question of blackness, black identity and equal rights, the headtie became for black women one of the most potent, subversive visual statements of the now global black-consciousness movement. The seemingly innocent function of what was just a length of cloth, qualified by its established profile as a humble utilitarian apparel, belied the headtie's subversive message of black-consciousness, and the acceptance of blackness as a cultural force, and finally Africa as the epicentre of black culture (figure 26). The headtie, the Afro and dreadlocks during this period, offered conscious black women throughout the African diaspora a solution to the tug of war between natural and artificial black hairstyles which engendered a duality of insecurity in black identity. Kobena Mercer has argued that the historical importance of the Afro and dreadlocks hairstyles provided a liberating and radical feature to black lives, 'they counter-politicized the signifier of ethnic devalorization, redefining blackness as a positive attribute',[32] but their incorporation into mainstream fashion in a short period of time depoliticised the hairstyles. The same fate befell the elegant headtie designs described above. These could be found on the fashion pages of such tomes of western high fashion as *Vogue* and *Harpers & Queen*. Nonetheless, the seed had been planted and the myriad African fabric designs, whirled into a crowning tower of glory by Rastafarian women from the mid-1970s in devout adherence to their religious teachings that a woman should not have her hair uncovered in public, redeemed the headtie from the realms of commercialisation, back into the traditions of African diaspora dress and identity. The headtie then, acquired the status of headdress; a simple or complex artistically arranged structure, permanent or temporary, intended for reuse and preservation. A headdress acts as a cultural or individual signifier of aesthetic improvement of appearance, mood reflections, honour, ethnic or sub-ethnic identities, disguise, protection, healing properties, transition and change of social personality, political or social and initiatory experiences.

What had filtered down to me in Doncaster was the resultant effects of the civil rights and Black Power movements from the 1950s to the 1970s. The movements were motivated into high-profile political action, to confront and redress the negation of African–American existence by white American society. To counteract this, African–Americans adopted pan-African ideology in the early 1970s to reclaim their cultural heritage and to sharpen the visibility of their 'new' identity. The skilfully blended elements of African cultural traditions and dress, with contemporary African–American trends, spread to Britain and Jamaica to create an African diaspora cultural- identity and aesthetic. With hindsight, my decision to follow the lead of other black women in Britain, Jamaica and America and to wear the headtie in public, was a subconscious way of participating in the advancement of black culture and politics. Here was an example of an individual identity born out of a collective identity. Due to strict matriarchal control, I was not allowed to be a vocal activist at the front line of the black-consciousness movement, only a silent supporter. Dress and my clothed body were the only tools I had for engagement with this transnational movement. Now I realise dress had empowered me to also become womanist, to take responsibility for and claim some level of control over my identity, by choosing to amplify my 'otherness'. Not until the

1980s and in my mid-twenties as a mature fashion student living in London, did I have the courage to wear the 'Mammy' style in public (often with men's secondhand suits) to define my own individual aesthetic diaspora identity. My practical training and experience to assemble and redefine the clothed body, to go to history and to draw on one's personal memory and image bank for potent and provocative symbols of cultural comment, equipped me with the impetus for such a personal transition. Hall has remarked that the production of a cultural identity is based on the retelling of the past, the imaginative rediscovery based on a shared culture, a 'Oneness' which underpins all other superficial differences; and the 'significance of difference' results in 'what we really are and become' due to the intervention of history, concepts focal to the empowerment and creativity of essentially marginalised and invisible people.[33] Cultural identity, an evolutionary force with a soul, exists, engaging the politics of identity into the broader cultural discourse. The formulation of a cultural identity by Black British females, as with African–American and Caribbean women, is not an unbroken line from some fixed origin,[34] but is framed by the cultural exchange within host societies, and between members of the African diaspora based on a shared experience, to legitimise the dual dynamic of the cultural identification of 'Black British'.

Notes

1 G. McCracken, *Culture and Consumption*, Indiana University Press, Indianapolis, 1990, p. 61.

2 P. Calefato, 'Fashion and Worldliness: Language and Imagery of the Clothed Body', in *Fashion Theory: Journal of Dress, Body & Culture*, 1:1, March 1997.

3 See L. Wright, 'Objectifying Gender: The Stiletto Heel', in P. Kirkham and J. Attfield (eds), *A View from The Interior*, London, The Women's Press, 1998; and selected works in P. Kirkham (ed.), *The Gendered Object*, Manchester, Manchester University Press, 1997.

4 A. Walker, *In Search of Our Mother's Gardens: A Womanist Prose*, London, The Women's Press, 1991, p. ix.

5 H. Charles, 'The Language of Womanism: Re-thinking Difference', in H. Safia Mirza (ed.), *Black British Feminism*, London, Routledge, 1997, pp. 280–4.

6 Maulana ron Karenga 1968 dictum quoted in P. Gilroy, *There Ain't No Black in the Union Jack*, London, Hutchinson, 1987, pp. 176–7.

7 D. G. Robin Kelley, 'Nap Time: Historicizing the Afro', in *Fashion Theory: Journal of Dress, Body & Culture*, 1:4, December 1997, p. 343. Kelley illustrates that 'that natural' hairstyle which became a symbol of the 1960s black political and cultural radicalism emerged among black middle-class and Bohemian women in the late 1950s.

8 R. Powell, *Black Art and Culture in the 20th Century*, London, Thames & Hudson, 1997, p. 121.

 9 V. Steele, 'Anti-Fashion: The 1970s', in *Fashion Theory: Journal of Dress, Body & Culture*, 1:3, September 1997, pp. 280–1.

10 *Ibid.*, p. 281.

11 *Ibid.*, p. 287.

12 There were exceptions. For example, Dorothy Dandrige was given more glamorous roles due to her fair complexion that enabled her to 'pass for a white person'. See also H. Bradley Foster, *'New Raiments of Self': African-American Clothing in the Ante-bellum South*, Oxford, Berg, 1997, pp. 293–9.

13 S. Bourne, 'Denying Her Place: Hattie McDaniel's Surprising Acts', in P. Cook and P. Dodd (eds), *Women and Film*, London, Scarlet Press, p. 30.

14 *Ibid.*, p. 31.

15 S. Hall, 'Cultural Identity and Diaspora', in J. Rutherford, *Identity: Community, Culture, Difference*, London, Lawrence and Wishart, 1990, pp. 235–6.

16 H. Bradley Griebel, 'The West African Origin of the African-American Headwrap', in J. B. Eicher (ed.), *Dress and Ethnicity*, Oxford, Berg, 1995, p. 216. Bradley Griebel confirms that the headwrap was a popular item of headwear among West African women from the mid-eighteenth century, following extensive trade expansion by Europe in Africa. Although she cannot verify how widely it was used, there is evidence of a West African woman in Cape Verde, now Senegal, who was adorned in a 'turban' as early as 1647.

17 See *ibid.*; also H. Bradley Griebel, 'New Raiments', in R. McDonald, *The Economy and Material Culture of Slaves: Goods and Chattels on the Sugar Plantations of Jamaica and Louisiana*, Baton Rouge and London, Louisiana State University, 1993.

18 P. Hunt, 'Swathed in Cloth: The Headwraps of Some African-American Women in Georgia and South Carolina During the Late Nineteenth and Early Twentieth Centuries', in *Dress: The Costume Society of America*, 21, 1994. I would like to thank Amy de la Haye for bringing this article to my attention.

19 See McDonald, *The Economy and Material Culture of Slaves*.

20 M. B. Caffin, *A Jamaica Outing*, Boston, Mass., The Sherwood Publishing Company, 1899.

21 The real madras handkerchief was handwoven in Madras, which distinguished it from the imitation madras handkerchief produced on power looms in Lancashire from the late eighteenth century onwards.

22 The date of its occurrence in the United States.

23 S. Lee Evenson, 'A History of Indian Madras Manufacture and Trade: Shifting Patterns of Exchange', unpublished Ph.D. thesis, p. 11.

24 The madras check is also associated with Jamaica, but from the research conducted to date the real and imitation Indian madras were the major imports.

25 W. D. Teague, *Design This Day: The Technique of Order in the Machine Age*, London, Studio, n.d., p. 51.

26 Calefato, 'Fashion and Worldliness', p. 72.

27 *Ibid.*, p. 72.

28 C. King, 'Making Things Mean: Cultural Representation in Objects', in F. Bonner, L. Goodman, R. Allen and C. Kink (eds), *Imagining Women: Cultural Representations and Gender*, London and Cambridge, Mass., Polity Press, 1992, p. 15.

29 See I. Kopytoff, 'The Cultural Biography of Things: Commoditization as Process', in A. Appadurai (ed.), *The Social Life of Things*; S. Ahmed, 'It's a Sun-tan, Isn't It?: Autobiography as an Identificatory Practice', in Safia Mirza (ed.), *Black British Feminism*.

30 Kopytoff, 'The Cultural Biography of Things', p. 90.

31 Ahmed, 'It's a Sun-tan, Isn't It?', pp. 151–5.

32 K. Mercer, 'Black Hair/Style Politics', *New Formations*, 3, winter 1987, pp. 40–1.

33 Hall, 'Cultural Identity and Diaspora', pp. 223–5.

34 *Ibid.*, p. 226.

6 ✧ Religious dress in Italy in the late Middle Ages

Cordelia Warr

IT is often not possible to define with accuracy religious dress during the late Middle Ages by examining fragments of original clothing. This is because very little still survives and also because we cannot be sure of how representative of the whole is that which remains.[1] Secondary sources must be used in order to put together a clear notion of the colour and form of the clothing used. In the case of nuns these sources consist of clothing regulations made in the relevant constitutions and of paintings showing exemplary members of the orders and their companions. Neither source can be considered as complete in itself. The two should be used in conjunction with one another to provide a better understanding of religious dress during this period. By concentrating on the relationship between written regulations describing dress and painted representations of it, we can begin to evaluate pictorial and documentary evidence.

This chapter will consider representations of, and regulations for, the Poor Clares and the Second Order of Saint Dominic. Both orders flourished from the beginning of the thirteenth century in the wake of the success of the Franciscan and Dominican male orders.[2] The Poor Clares formed around Saint Clare of Assisi who ran away from her home to join Saint Francis and was eventually installed in the restored convent buildings of San Damiano, just outside Assisi, with others who wanted to follow her example.[3] The foundation of San Damiano was quickly followed by a number of other houses of nuns who took their inspiration from Clare and Francis. Jacques de Vitry records that there were various convents of Poor Clares by 1216. A list dated 1228 names twenty-three houses in Italy and it is possible that by 1400 there were approximately two hundred and fifty.[4] The history of the female branch of the Dominicans is somewhat different. The first house of Dominican nuns, that of Prouille, was co-founded by Dominic himself.[5] By the time of the death of the Saint there were two other houses under the care of his friars, San Sisto in Rome as well as a convent in Madrid, and plans for a convent in Bologna.[6]

The formation of new religious orders was problematical at this time due to the regulations of the Lateran Council of 1215 which prohibited new religious rules. Canon XIII of the Council stated that diversity in religious practice produced confusion and because of this, decreed that no one was to found a new order.[7] In effect this meant that new orders were still founded but had to take previously formulated rules. Certain things, such as the habit, could be chosen separately and this was one of the means used to differentiate the new orders.

The rule given to the Poor Clares in order to be in line with Lateran regulations was that of Saint Benedict. However, in the first fifty years of the Order's existence the constitutions surrounding the rule were altered a number of times. Five different versions had been put into effect by 1263. The first was the formula given to Clare by Saint Francis and later supplemented by the Constitutions of Cardinal Ugolino. In 1247 Innocent IV expanded on the previous regulations in his bull *Cum omnis vera religio* of 6 August. Six years later in 1253, Saint Clare's own rule was approved in the bull *Solet annuere* of 9 August and in 1259 Alexander IV confirmed the rule of Longchamp which, however, did not have a great impact in Italy.[8] The final, but not definitive, rule given to the Order was that of Urban IV, *Beata Clara Virtute Clarens*, of 18 October 1263.[9]

The situation was similar for the Dominican Second Order. The final and official constitutions for the Dominican Second Order were put into force in 1259, four years before Urban IV's final attempt to impose uniformity on the Poor Clares.[10] The first known rule for the Second Order is that formulated for the convent of San Sisto in Rome and this was to be the template for subsequent rules. The rule is not known in its original form but in that published by Gregory IX in a bull of 23 October 1232.[11] Following this was the rule written for the nuns at Montargis sometime after 1244 by the then Provincial of France, Humbert of Romans.[12] This became the basis of the definitive rule promulgated in 1259 and also drawn up by Humbert of Romans. After becoming Master General at the General Chapter at Buda in 1254, Humbert embarked on a reform of the rule and government of the Dominican nuns. He sought, as the Franciscans and successive popes were already trying to do for the Second Order of Saint Francis, but with more success, to ensure that the same version of the rule was followed by all houses belonging to the Order. This uniformity was to include dress. Having ordered the provincial priors to send to the following Chapter details of the nunneries that they had accepted under their jurisdiction he proceeded to draw up a new set of constitutions with the support of the pope, Alexander IV. These constitutions were published at the 1259 Chapter General and it was at the same time made clear that any convent which did not accept them without question was no longer to be considered part of the Order. These measures to a large extent prevented the difference in usages which was the bane of those who attempted to govern the Clares.[13]

Like other aspects of the rule of a particular order, those regarding clothing tended to evolve rather than emerge fully-fledged. In some cases, clothing usages can be followed through a series of regulations which reacted to needs and abuses as they arose. The main items of clothing used by nuns at this time were a long tunic over which could be worn a scapular. The scapular, which drew its name from the Latin word for the shoulder blades, was worn over the shoulders and covered the back and front of the wearer, very much like an apron.[14] It was a protective garment often intended for use when the nun was working.[15] In addition to this was the cloak or mantle and the veil.[16] While other parts of the habit could be considered the outward sign of the order, the presence and colour of the veil was the sign of full or partial entry into the religious life.[17] From early Christian times it had been customary to veil consecrated virgins.[18] However, the early monastic rules for women did not enumerate the clothes to be used by the nuns. This is the case with the regulations composed by Waldebertus, Aurelianus and Caesarius of Arles for example.[19]

When compared to the rules just mentioned, the first set of instructions for the Poor Clares, that of Cardinal Ugolino, is much more specific. His clothing prescriptions state that,

> Everyone is to have two tunics and one mantle … The scapular should be of a light/religious cloth, or linsey-woolsey if they want, of a suitable width and length, as the quality and dimensions of each (nun) requires, which is to be worn when they are working, or when they are doing anything which does not permit of wearing a cloak. If, however, they want to wear it at the same time as the cloak, or even to sleep with it, they are by no means forbidden (to do so). They may also, from time to time, not wear it, if this seems proper to the abbess, due to great heat, or any other reason for which it would be oppressive to wear it.[20]

Cardinal Ugolino deals with clothes in a practical manner but by no means one that implies complete uniformity of colour or cut, nor one that gives the opportunity for it. Noticeably absent is any mention of the veil or of the colour of the habit. There is a considerable amount of choice left to the nuns and abbesses as to what should be allowed within a particular convent: such as that the nuns may wear a scapular 'if they want'.

The rule formulated by Saint Clare, and followed at Assisi, makes little mention of the dress of the sisters.[21] This is mainly to stress that the garments should always be poor and to give instructions on the number of garments that the sisters could have at any one time.[22] No further details were provided. However, unlike Ugolino, Saint Clare does mention the veil, although not its form or colour. She orders that no sister should be veiled during the time of her probation.[23]

Innocent IV's regulations, six years earlier in 1247, contain the first mention of the rope that the Clares wore around the waist in place of a belt.[24] This was to be worn only by fully professed nuns, those who had taken their final and solemn vows, as was the black veil. The statues further state both the number of tunics that each nun may have and the material to be used as well as mentioning the scapular, as did Ugolino's 'forma di vita'.[25] The final rule for the Poor Clares, that of Urban IV, makes only one main addition to Innocent's *Cum omnis vera religio*. It orders that the habit is to be of a colour that is 'neither completely white nor completely black'.[26] This is the first time that a rule for the Clares had made any specifications regarding colour. However it still left scope for considerable diversity between shades of brown and grey.

Both the Urbanist rule and that of Innocent IV gave a significant amount of attention to the veil: the white veil worn by the lay sisters whose job it was to assist in the day-to-day running of the convent, and by the novices who had not yet taken their final vows, and the white wimple that the fully professed sisters wore under their black veil. For the fully professed nuns this veil took the form of a piece of cloth arranged in such a way as to cover the forehead, the cheeks, the neck and the throat.[27] For the lay sisters it was a piece of white cloth sufficient to cover the shoulders and the breast.[28]

Even the unprecedented detail of the Urbanist regulations is still not sufficient to enable us to envisage with accuracy the appearance of the wimple or the other items that went to make up the habit. In the many paintings of this period showing Saint Clare, the white wimple frequently became two veils – one used to cover the neck, forehead and cheeks, and another piece of white cloth laid on top of it which can be seen beneath the black veil. These were not always used together. There is a wimple without the white underveil in a fifteenth-century representation of Saint Clare in a panel by Sano di Pietro in the Pinacoteca Nazionale in Siena (figure 27).[29] This follows to the letter the decrees of Urban IV. Simone Martini, however, depicts Saint Clare with both a wimple and a white underveil in the fresco from the soffit of the entrance arch to the Saint Martin Chapel in the Lower Church of San Francesco in Assisi, painted between 1312 and 1319 (figure 28).[30] Saint Clare's wimple covers her forehead, as prescribed in the rule of 1263, but not her cheeks or neck.

Regional differences were allowed for in some versions of the constitutions of the Poor Clares. For example, in Clare's rule she states that clothes should be provided according to the places in which the convents

27   Sano di Pietro, *Saint Clare of Assisi and Elizabeth of Hungary*,
Pinacoteca Nazionale, Siena

were founded, the conditions and the temperature.[31] The most striking regional difference was in the Veneto where, in representations of the fourteenth and fifteenth centuries, a striped mantle is usually shown. For example, in the early fourteenth-century polyptych, the *Coronation of the Virgin* in the Accademia, Venice, Paolo Veneziano represents a striped cloak in the scene of Saint Francis giving Saint Clare her monastic dress. Another example is in the slightly earlier central panel of the Trieste triptych in the Museo Sartori in Trieste depicting the *Death of Saint Clare* (figure 29).[32] It was probably common for members of a particular order not to wear the prescribed habit. In the second half of the fifteenth century for example, the questions sent to monasteries by the Vallombrosan Master General asked whether the monks wore the habit of their Order.[33] However, the use of the striped mantle is so widespread and so well publicised pictorially that it cannot be accounted for merely as disobedience to the constitutions.[34] That it cannot be explained by reference to any of the constitutions governing the Clares is evidence only of the lack of specific detail in the regulations, rather than of disobedience to them.

If we are to judge from pictorial representation, the dress of the

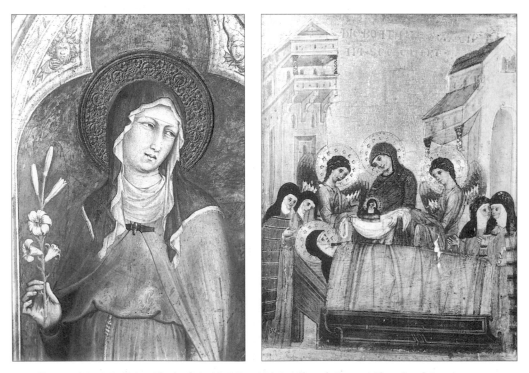

28   Simone Martini, *Saint Clare of Assisi*, Saint Martin Chapel, Lower Church of San Francesco, Assisi

29   Master of the Saint Clare Triptych, *The Death of Saint Clare*, Museo Sartori, Trieste

Dominican Second Order was not subject to regional changes of the magnitude of those found within the Poor Clares. The dress regulations of the Dominican nuns are well documented and at first sight the problems encountered would appear to be similar to those of the Poor Clares. The Dominicans also had to take a previously existing rule – that attributed to Saint Augustine – and adapt certain parts of it, including dress, for their own needs. The habit of the Second Order consists of a white tunic and scapular with a black cloak and veil. It closely mirrors that of the male Dominicans said to have been given to them by the Virgin who appeared to one of their number, Reginald, and after having cured him of his ills, bestowed the habit on him.[35] The first Dominican nuns in Prouille and at San Sisto in Rome probably wore a white habit.[36] Each of the successive constitutions provided instructions on the type of habit to be worn by the nuns, the number of tunics permitted and the type of cloth to be used. However, there is very little detail regarding the colour of the various items of clothing and the exact form that they were to take. None of the rules mention what form the veil was to take before and after profession, both of which are specifically enumerated in the Urbanist rule for the Clares. It is only Humbert's regulations for the sisters of Montargis that stipulates the colour of the habit: a black cloak and a white tunic.[37] The earlier regulations for San Sisto say that the habit should be white, while Humbert's definitive version of 1259 does not mention colour.[38] Otherwise the main point which is insisted upon is the scapular: present in all three constitutions and especially emphasised in that of 1259 which orders that the scapular be shorter than the tunic and that the sisters should always wear it.[39]

A female Dominican commissioner can be seen in a fresco of the early fifteenth century in the church of San Sisto Vecchio in Rome (figure 30).[40] The fresco, on the left wall of the nave near the apse, is divided into three areas, the first two of which show scenes from the life of Saint Catherine of Siena.[41] In the central area a kneeling nun to the right of Christ was almost certainly the commissioner of the scene. Catherine, to the left of the central area, wears the habit of the Third Order of Saint Dominic: a white veil and tunic with a black cloak. The fully professed nun is identified by her black veil.[42]

From an examination of some of the representations and regulations of the Poor Clares and the Dominicans it is clear that the appearance of the habit cannot be accurately gauged using only one of the above sources. There are a number of instances in which the painted representation gives a much more detailed, if not necessarily more accurate, account of the clothes worn by the members of these Orders. The cord that the Poor Clares wore around the waist, for instance, although mentioned only in the regulations promulgated by Innocent IV in 1247 and Urban IV in 1263 can be seen much earlier in paintings representing members of the Order. The early fourteenth-century panel, the *Death of Saint Clare*, mentioned above, shows the cord worn by the nun on the left (figure 29). The same item was painted by Simone Martini in the Saint Martin Chapel in the second decade of the fourteenth century (figure 28). Moreover, in both paintings the cord is knotted in the same manner as the cord used by the Franciscans. The knots are never mentioned in the rules, either for the Clares or the Franciscans, yet they are universally attested to in painting.[43] A similar instance is the use of the scapular. None of the paintings mentioned representing Clare or members of her order show the scapular. The regulations formulated by Cardinal Ugolino, Innocent IV and Urban IV all refer to the scapular as a piece of clothing to be worn while working. Saint Clare's own rule does not refer to a scapular at all but rather to a small mantle to be used for the same purpose.[44] In the case of the Dominican Second Order the scapular was obligatory yet it is not always clearly visible in paintings of members of the Order. The central area of the fresco in San Sisto in Rome shows a kneeling commissioner apparently not wearing a scapular (figure 30).

30 Scenes showing Saint Catherine of Siena, San Sisto Vecchio, Rome

31 Simone de' Crocefissi, *Saint Helen and the True Cross*,
Pinacoteca Nazionale, Bologna

These examples indicate that to evaluate fully the form of the religious dress of an order both written and painted evidence must be taken into account. A close reading of both 'texts' is necessary to avoid possible confusion. There are a number of cases where the dividing line between the habits of various orders is obscured. One documented example from outside Italy is revealing. In England, the *Mappa Mundi* dating from the beginning of the thirteenth century provides a list of women's convents and also gives some indication of the order to which the communities belonged. However, the arrangement is simply in terms of colour, with the nuns being described as black or white. Nuns described as white could have belonged to a number of orders and Cistercian nuns, for example, could be described as either black or white depending on the convent from which they came.[45] The same diversity of habit was actually provided for in the rule of the Premonstratensian nuns. The statutes for the Order prescribe the clothes of the nuns which were to be white *except* where the custom of the place made another colour necessary.[46]

Such variations in the descriptions of the habit and in the regulations for it, in addition to the frequent lack of detail, throw up some interesting questions. A painting from the last years of the fourteenth century by Simone de' Crocefissi in the Pinacoteca Nazionale in Bologna shows *Saint Helen and the True Cross* (figure 31). At the Saint's feet is the donor in the garb of a nun. The commissioner wears a white tunic over which is a black mantle. On her head is a white wimple partially covered by a white cowl and over this a black veil. The subject of the painting has led to the suggestion that it was commissioned for the convent of Sant'Elena in Bologna which was Augustinian and was only later transferred to the Dominican convent of Sant'Agnese from whence it was taken during the Napoleonic suppression.[47] The nun would therefore be a member of the Augustinian Order. The lengthy inscription gives no clues to the religious sympathies of the commissioner.[48] Although the subject matter points towards the convent of Sant'Elena the habit of the donor does not. The white tunic and black mantle of the nun kneeling in an attitude of prayer to the left-hand side seems to be an indication of her attachment to the Dominican Order. They conform to the statutes of Humbert of Romans for the sisters at Montargis and later adapted for the whole of the Second Order.[49] However, just as in the example from San Sisto Vecchio already mentioned, the scapular, if there is one, is not shown. Furthermore, there is the extremely unusual addition of the cowl. This is not mentioned in any of the regulations for Dominican nuns although it was known monastic practice sometimes to have a cowl attached to the scapular.[50] As such it was specifically forbidden in the regulations of Innocent IV and Urban IV for the Poor Clares.[51] Thus, in this case, the evidence is inconclusive.

Neither the inscription, nor the representation of religious dress, nor the iconography of the painting can be used to provide incontrovertible proof of the provenance of the work: there are only indications on which to base hypotheses.

The possibilities for diversity of habit within the Poor Clares and the Second Order of Saint Dominic are striking both in the various rules formulated for the two Orders during the thirteenth century and in paintings showing their members. The regulations tend to demonstrate, in their first versions, a lack of detail in the enumeration and description of clothing appropriate for the nuns. Subsequent adaptations, while they are more specific, still often lack the descriptive detail needed if a present-day historian is to reconstruct them with accuracy. The paintings both elucidate and clarify the appearance of the habit, yet they also pose questions of their own. There are cases where the habit shown does not conform to the regulations and also examples where it drastically departs from them. To this must be added one further element in the equation: that of the artist, his training and personal style, as well as his ability or desire to provide the viewer with a copy of the habit either as worn or as it was intended to be worn. It is, to give one example, easy to imagine that Simone Martini, in the Lower Church at Assisi, may have been tempted to sacrifice a little truth in the interests of a flowing Gothic line (figure 28). Yet with all these provisos, knowledge of the religious habit during the Later Middle Ages is much enhanced by the use of painted and written sources in association with one another.

Notes

1 H. M. Zylstra-Zweens, *Of His Array Telle I no Lenger Tale: Aspects of Costume, Arms and Armour in Western Europe 1200–1400*, Amsterdam, 1988, p. 3.

2 For a brief history of the origins and foundation of the Franciscan Order, see J. Moorman, *A History of the Franciscan Order from its Origins to the Year 1517*, Oxford, 1968, pp. 3–31. For the Dominican Order, see *Dizionario degli Istituti di Perfezione*, diretto da G. Pellicia & G. Rocca, Rome, 1977, 8 vols, vol. IV, cols 923 ff.; also R. F. Bennett, *The Early Dominicans: Studies in Thirteenth-Century Dominican History*, Cambridge, 1937, p. 22, n. 1.

3 Moorman, *Franciscan Order*, pp. 33–4 for the founding of San Damiano. For further information on the foundation of the Poor Clares, *ibid.*, pp. 32–9.

4 Moorman, *Franciscan Order*, pp. 38–9, 406–7.

5 E. T. Brett, *Humbert of Romans: His Life and Views of Thirteenth-Century Society*, Toronto, 1984, p. 58.

6 Brett, *Humbert of Romans*, pp. 58–9.

7 G. R. Galbraith, *The Constitutions of the Dominican Order 1216–1360* (Manchester, 1925), p. 33.

8 The convent of Longchamp was founded by Isabelle, sister of Saint Louis. The main impact of its rule was in England and France. Moorman, *Franciscan Order*, p. 213.

9 M. de Fontette, *Les Religieuses à l'Âge Classique du Droit Canon*, Paris, 1967, pp. 142–8.

10 *Ibid.*, p. 99.

11 *Ibid.*, p. 92.

12 Brett, *Humbert of Romans*, p. 75; R. Creytens, 'Les Constitutions Primitives des Sœurs Dominicaines de Montargis', *Archivum Fratrum Praedicatorum*, XVII, 1947, p. 56.

13 Brett, *Humbert of Romans*, pp. 71–3.

14 *Dizionario degli Istituti di Perfezione*, vol. VIII, cols 1015–18.

15 Saint Benedict, for example, considered it as such in his rule for monks. *Dizionario degli Istituti di Perfezione*, vol. VIII, col. 1015.

16 *Ibid.*, vol. I, cols 55–6.

17 *Ibid.*, vol. I, col. 57. Also *Catholic Encyclopaedia vol. XIV*, 1981 Palatine, Illinois (reprint of 1967), p. 590.

18 Tertullian, 'On the Veiling of Virgins', in A. Roberts and J. Donaldson (eds), *Translations of the Writings of the Fathers down to AD 325*, vol. 18, Edinburgh, 1870, pp. 154–80.

19 *Patrologia Latina*, J. P. Migne (ed.), Paris, 1854, vol. 88, cols 1053–70, *ibid.*, vol. 68, cols 399–406, M. C. McCarthy, *The Rule for the Nuns of Caesarius of Arles: A Translation with a Critical Introduction*, Washington, DC, 1960, p. 185.

20 See G. Salvi, 'La regola di San Benedetto nei primordi dell'ordine di Santa Chiara', *Benedictina*, VIII fasc. I–IV, 1954, pp. 84–5.

21 Moorman, *Franciscan Order*, p. 213.

22 *Fontes Francescani*, a cura di E. Menestò e S. Brufani, Assisi, 1995, pp. 2293–4.

23 'Nulla infra tempus probationis veletur' Menestò, *Fontes*, p. 2294.

24 J. H. Sbaralea, *Bullarium Franciscanum*, vol. I, Rome, 1759, p. 478, 'Pro cingulo autem chordam habeant'.

25 *Ibid.*, p. 478, 'Unaquaeque soror, praeter cilicium, vel stamineum, si habuerit duas tunicas' etc.

26 J. H. Sbaralea, *Bullarium Franciscanum*, vol. II, Rome, 1761, p. 509. 'Tunicae quoque superiores, scapularia et mantelli coloris omnino albi vel nigri aliquatenus non ferantur.'

27 *Ibid.*, p. 511. 'Vittis aut velis de panno communi omnino albis non tamen pretiosus, aut curiosus capita sua cooperiant uniformiter, et honeste, ita quod frons, genae et collum, et gula sint cooperta.'

28 *Ibid.*

29 P. Torriti, *La Pinacoteca Nazionale di Siena. I dipinti*, Genoa, 1990, p. 561. Sano di Pietro was born in 1406 and died in 1481. The saint is here erroneously identified as Giuliana despite the presence of companion panels from the same, now dismembered, altarpiece showing Saints Francis and Louis of Toulouse and despite the fact that she is wearing the habit of the Poor Clares. Her companion, wearing a white veil, must be Saint Elizabeth of Hungary, who was considered to be the first member of the Franciscan Third Order, carrying the miraculous flowers referred

to in her legend. G. Kaftal, *The Iconography of the Saints in the Central and South Italian Schools of Painting*, Florence, 1965, col. 381.

30 A. Martindale, *Simone Martini*, Oxford, 1988, pp. 174–5, 178.

31 'Secundum ... loca et tempora et frigidas', Menestò, *Fontes*, p. 2294. Cardinal Ugolino's 'forma di vita' says only that there is no need to wear the scapular if it is too hot: Salvi, *San Benedetto*, pp. 84–5. The same clause is to be found in Innocent IV's regulations and in those of Urban IV of 1263: *Bullarium Franciscanum*, vol. I, p. 478 and *Bullarium Franciscanum*, vol. II, p. 511.

32 S. Moschini Marconi, *Gallerie dell'Accademia di Venezia: Opere d'Arte dei Secoli XIV e XV*, Rome, 1955, p. 15; C. Travi, 'Il Maestro del Trittico di Santa Chiara. Appunti per la Pittura Veneto del Primo Trecento', *Arte Cristiana*, 749, 1992, pp. 81–96.

33 G. A. Bruckner, 'Monasteries, Friaries and Nunneries in Quattrocento Florence', in *Christianity and the Renaissance: Image and Religious Imagination in the Quattrocento*, T. Verdon and J. Henderson (eds), New York, 1990, pp. 41–62. This reference, p. 55.

34 C. Warr, *Bad Habits in Trieste: The Striped Mantle of the Poor Clares*, Arte Cristiana, 789, 1999, pp. 415–30.

35 C. Warr, *Laying Claim to Clothing: The Vision of the Blessed Reginald of Orléans and the Visual Importance of the Habit of the Dominican Order from the Thirteenth to the Fifteenth Century* (forthcoming).

36 Fontette, *Les Religieuses*, page 94, n. 30. The rule of San Sisto is only known from a later bull of Gregory IX dated 23 October 1232. T. Ripoll, *Bullarium Ordinis Fratrum Praedicatorum*, vol. VII, Rome, 1739, pp. 410–13.

37 R. Creytens, 'Les Constitutions Primitives des Sœurs Dominicaines de Montargis', *Archivum Fratrum Praedicatorum*, XVII, 1947, pp. 41–82. Clothing regulations are contained in Chapter X, p. 72, the first sentence of which reads, 'Vestes laneas, honestas et albas et non nimius preciosas deferent sorores, praeter mantellum quod debet esse nigrum'.

38 The rule of San Sisto states that 'Vestes autem sint albae ...'. *Bullarium Ordinis Praedicatorum*, vol. VII, p. 411. For Humbert of Romans's Rule of 1259, see *Analecta Sacri Ordinis Fratrum Praedicatorum*, III, 1897, pp. 337–48.

39 *Ibid.*, p. 341, 'scapularia vero sine quibus non vadant sint tunicis breviora'.

40 S. Romano, *Eclissi di Roma: Pittura Murale a Roma e nel Lazio da Bonifacio VIII a Martino V (1295–1431)*, Rome, 1992, p. 411.

41 The episode from Saint Catherine's life to which the frescoes refer can be found in *Acta Sanctorum*, April III, Paris, 1866, p. 896, nos 35–8. It is also related in G. Kaftal, *Saint Catherine in Tuscan Painting*, Oxford, 1949, pp. 53–6.

42 The rule for the Third Order of Saint Dominic is printed in G. G. Meersseman, *Ordo Fraternitatis: Confraternite e Pietà dei laici nel medioevo*, vol I, Rome, 1977, p. 401.

43 C. Frugoni, *Francesco e l'Invenzione delle Stimmate: Una Storia per Parole e Immagini fino a Bonaventura e Giotto*, Turin, 1993, p. 276.

44 Menestò, *Fontes*, p. 2294, 'Mantellulas etiam possint sorores habere pro allevatione et honestate servitu et laboris'.

45 S. Thompson, *Women Religious: The Founding of English Nunneries after the Norman Conquest*, Oxford, 1991, pp. 100–2.

46 Fontette, *Les Religieuses*, p. 23.

47 A. Emiliani, *La Pinacoteca Nazionale di Bologna: Catologo generale delle opere esposte*, Bologna, 1987, p. 29.

48 G. Kaftal and F. Bisogni, *The Iconography of the Saints in the Painting of North-East Italy*, Oxford, 1978, cols 396–402.

49 See n. 36 above.

50 *Dizionario degli Istituti di Perfezione*, vol. VIII, col. 1015.

51 For the rule of Innocent IV see *Bullarium Franciscanum*, vol. I, p. 478: 'Habeant et scapularia sine caputio de vili, et religioso panno …'. For that of Urban IV see *Bullarium Franciscanum*, vol. II, p. 511, where the same phrase is used.

7 ✧ The mantua: its evolution and fashionable significance in the seventeenth and eighteenth centuries

Avril Hart

T HE evolution of the woman's mantua is associated with a significant change in fashionable dress in the last quarter of the seventeenth century. As a fashion, it coincided with the long awaited emancipation of seamstresses who were finally allowed to acquire professional status as dressmakers, or mantua makers as they eventually became known. Mantua maker became the generic term for all dressmakers until the beginning of the twentieth century. The use of the name is an indication of the importance of the mantua in the history of women's fashions: it was the first major item of dress made by women for women.

Until the late seventeenth century, men tailors had adopted certain protective practices to prevent women, the seamstresses, from making any of the outer clothes for their own sex. Specific restrictions had been imposed so that women's area of expertise only extended to making items of linen and lightweight silks and gauzes. These were garments of simple construction yet required a high degree of needlework skills and techniques. They included all undergarments, shirts chemises, and neckwear such as ruffs and cravats of linen or lace and unstructured garments like hoods made of thin silks or gauzes, as well as household linens. The tailors claimed that by imposing these regulations they were protecting their own livelihoods as breadwinners for their families. Randle Holme in his book, *The Academy of Armory and Blazon*, published in 1688, gives a complete list of items made by seamstresses – note that the mantua was already being made by the seamstress/dressmaker at the date of publication:

Shirt, or Shift for a Man
Smock or Womans Shift
Ruffs, pleated Bands of two or three heights
Round Robins, narrow Ruffs only about the Doublet Collar
Foulds, Sets, Ruffles
Cravatts. Half shirts

32   Mantua and matching petticoat of brocaded silk, English 1733–34

Cuffs or sleeve cuffs
Ruffles for the hands, both Plain and Laced
Sleeves.
Handkerchiefs for Womens Necks, both round and square
Whisks, to be worn with a gown
Shapes for Mantuas
Tuckers, or dresses (Note: Modesty in-fills for the décolletage)
Gorgetts, round Dresses plaited to be deep about Womens Necks
    (Note: ditto)
A Roman Dress, the Mantua cut square behind and round before
Night Rails or Cover-sluts
Women's Head Dresses
Quoifs. Chin-cloth. Caul. Chapparoon, Crossett, or Crosscloth
A Pinner is with long flaps hanging down the side of the cheeks
Hoods, made of either Gaues, Alamode, Lutestring, Sarsenet,
    Ducape, Vinian Sarsenet, Persia, India Silk, or Gaues and Birds Eye
    flowered [1]

The period of significant change covers the 1660s and 1670s, which
was a time of great social and political change particularly in Britain, with
the return to a monarchy and the reign of Charles II in 1660 after a
decade of the Commonwealth under Oliver Cromwell. One of the benefits
of the Restoration was the revival of the theatre and the new comedies
satirising contemporary society and fashions. Playwrights such as William
Wycherley (1640?–1716), Aphra Benn (1640?–89) and George Etherege
(1635?–91) all made comments on dress and of men and women who
were dedicated followers of fashion.

At this time the outer garments for women made by men tailors
consisted of a tightly fitted and boned, corset bodice, a rich silk outer
petticoat and an equally rich overskirt. Making the corset bodice continued
to be the prerogative of tailors. It was during this period that the seamstresses expanded their expertise to include a new informal garment known
as a nightgown which was similar in shape and style to that worn by
men. It is probable that the nightgown developed into the earliest of the
outer garments made by seamstresses. Although it seems inconceivable that
prior to this date women did not make their own clothes, the tailors'
restrictions were really applicable to the making of fashionable dress. Poorer
women must have made some of their own garments. Women who lived
in the country relied upon the travelling Petty Chapmen to bring textiles
and haberdashery for them to make clothes and household goods although
it is likely that even they had to rely upon a local tailor to make their
heavier woollen garments and men's clothing. A flourishing ready-made
and secondhand clothing market served the requirements of the less

affluent. In France, restrictions enforced by the men tailors on seamstresses appear to have been more rigid: it was not until 1675 that French seamstresses finally succeeded with their repeated petitions to Louis XIV for the right to make their own clothes. Finally, it was agreed that men tailors should continue to make certain items of dress for children of either sex until they reached eight years old and women's trained over-skirts for gowns and boned corsets for women as well as men's clothes.

The fashionable shape of the boned corset bodice in the decade 1660–70 was characterised by a wide, oval-shaped neckline, sloping shoulders and a slender body tapering to a narrow waist. Most corsets were laced down the centre back. The corset was constructed so that the centre front was curved inwards, pushing in the stomach and pushing up the bust. The vogue for a slender form became increasingly fashionable as the century progressed and to achieve this desirable shape the corset continued to deepen at the centre front and back and extended over the hips where it was slit to the waistline to form tabs which spread out comfortably over the hips. The fashion allowed the centre front tab to be worn outside the skirt or petticoat but the remaining tabs were tucked underneath the skirt waistband. The curved shape of the centre front was retained by inserting a busk (a shaped piece of wood, metal, bone or ivory) between the layers of fabric. The wide neckline curved up to the shoulders where the shoulder pieces or straps barely covered the tops of the shoulders; however, modesty was more or less retrieved by the addition of sleeves.

A daunting, contemporary description of the busk is given in the *Academy of Armory and Blazon*:

> A Busk, it is a strong piece of Wood, or Whalebone thrust down the middle of the Stomacher, to keep it streight and in compass, that the Breast nor Belly shall not swell too much out. These Buskes are usually made in length according to the necessity of the persons wearing it: if to keep in the fullness of the Breasts, then it extends to the Navel: if to keep the Belly down, then it reacheth to the Honor.[2]

Donneau de Vizé[3] noted in 1672 that ladies were wearing corsets so long in the waist that they came almost down to the thighs when the wearer had slender hips. As this was an outer garment the fashionable bodices were covered in rich silks and decorated with a selection of colourful lace, braids, ribbons or fly-braids. A chemise was worn under the bodice and was the first garment next to the skin. Any lace ruffles or frills were sewn to the neck band and cuffs of the chemise and removed for washing. Several layers of under petticoats were worn and the last and outer petticoat would normally be a very rich silk or patterned velvet with little decoration, or a plain silk richly decorated with flounces or lace, braids and fringes. The fashions of the 1670s were derived from the decade 1650–60 when an overskirt, with braid down the centre front edges and hem, was worn over the rich petticoat. The overskirt was open at the front with the edges meeting, but as the wearer moved glimpses of the rich petticoat became visible. As a rule, the corset bodice and overskirt were of matching fabrics while the petticoat was in complete contrast not only in colour but also technique. The corset and overskirt, for example, were of silk or silk velvet while the petticoat was of embroidered silk. The overskirt was set with cartridge pleats at the waist and tied about the waist with ribbons at the centre front and tucked under the centre tab of the corset so that the tips of the bows appeared beneath the tab.

From the 1660s to the 1670s, the overskirt widened at the front allowing the petticoat to remain visible, forming an inverted 'V' and the skirt lengthened to become a train. Although it is a visually pleasing shape, a train is a physically difficult item of dress to manoeuvre and various measures were soon adopted to cope with the weight of this encumbrance. The open fronts of the overskirt were draped to the sides and at the hips, revealing even more of the petticoat, the drapery was held in place by buttoned loops or jewelled clasps, the train itself was usually pinned up at the back to protect it from becoming soiled when out walking. All these features are recorded in paintings and sculptures of the period and in contemporary fashion plates. The treatment of the trained overskirt played a significant part in the evolution of the mantua and was to become an important feature of this style. But some radical changes had to take place before the mantua became a recognisable style. The term mantua, according to the *OED*, derives from manteau which is a corruption of the place-name Mantua in Italy, renowned for its fine silks. Mantua maker became the generic term for a dressmaker and continued in use until the early twentieth century, long after mantuas ceased to be worn. Recognisable descriptions of mantuas appearing in contemporary sources are fairly rare but Samuel Pepys mentions a new fashion for women, which had been described to him by Lady Jemimah, in his diary on 15 October 1666: 'the ladies are to go into a new fashion shortly; and that is to wear short coats above their anckles – which she nor I do not like, but conclude this long Trayne to be mighty graceful'.[4] The short coats referred to by Pepys could be one of the early appearances of the mantua. Randle Holme also describes the mantua as a short coat-like garment 'A Mantua, is a kind of loose Coat without any stayes in it ... but the skirt is sometimes no longer than the Knees others have them down to the Heels';[5] he also describes a similar garment called the Samare, 'This is a kind of loose garment without and stiffe Bodies under them, and was a great fashion for Women about the

year 1676. Some called them Mantuas, they have very short sleeves, nay
some of the Gallants of the times, have the Sleeves gathered up to the
top of the Shoulders and there stayed, or fastened with a Button or Loope,
or set with a rich Jewel'.[6]

There are portraits of this period which show women wearing a type
of loose gown with short looped-up sleeves and with the fronts of their
skirts turned back and pinned behind to reveal the lining. This new fashion
exchanged the ensemble of cumbersome corset bodice and outer petticoat
with a trained overskirt for a simpler one-piece garment (the mantua)
worn over a corset and outer petticoat, creating in one garment a similar
style and silhouette to that of the earlier and more complex fashion. The
new garment is thought to have originated from the *robe de chambre*, a
loosely cut gown for women worn as informal dress, which appeared in
the 1660s and 1670s (figure 33, *Femme de qualité en déshabillé sortant du
lit*, 1694 (Jean de St Jean)). It was a kimono-like gown, open down the
front, fastened by a sash and worn over a corset and outer petticoat. It was
the female counterpart to the man's nightgown which appeared at the same
time (figure 34, The doll Lady Clapham's *robe de chambre* (1690–1700)).

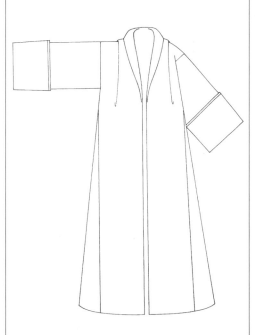

33 *Femme de qualité en déshabillé sortant du lit*, 1694 (Jean de St Jean)

34 Lady Clapham's *robe de chambre*, 1690–1700

This is known as a T-shaped garment (when laid out flat the T-shape is clear), because of its shape and simple construction, which may also be compared to men's shirts and women's chemises. As none of the first mantuas appear to have survived, their cut and construction is open to conjecture, with the only visual information taken from mantuas portrayed in contemporary paintings and engravings.

The cut and construction of surviving mantuas of the early eighteenth century show an affinity with the seventeenth-century nightgown, they have a centre-front opening from neck to hem, a trained skirt and short full sleeves with turned-back cuffs. However, the complete ensemble has a distinct resemblance to the earlier style of corset bodice and trained petticoat. For in its earliest stages in the 1660s and 1670s, the seamstress was attempting to create the contemporary fashionable silhouette without the help of the tailor. The easiest approach was to make a coat-like garment constructed along the same lines as a chemise and the nearest equivalent to that was the nightgown, a garment with which they were quite familiar. It is entirely possible that the idea for the mantua was derived from the morning dress of *en déshabillé* when women probably began to pin back the front skirts of the nightgown for convenience when engaged in some activity more energetic than sitting at a dressing table. This would conform to the current fashion of the pinned-back overskirt and reveal the outer petticoat at the same time. The whole ensemble would have been easier to wear and gave, at the same time, an air of casual elegance. New fashions are often derived from informal dress which gradually drifts into more fashionable forms and richer fabrics. The first fitting and shaping of the bodice was probably achieved by pleating the fabric to shape on the body then stitching it in place afterwards. The whole appearance would have been completed by a narrow buckled belt at the waist which would also hold the fronts in place and prevent the train from pulling the front of the gown open.

It was possible to buy ready-made mantuas as well as other clothes. Margaret Spufford in her book, *The Great Reclothing of Rural England*, provides the examples of two Kentish salesmen; Robert Amsden of Canterbury, who died in 1703, had included in his inventory some ready-made mantuas, which also implied that there was some kind of standard sizing being practised, '12 Women's damaske Mantues at 8s apiece £4 16s'.[7] The second example was that of John Wood of Sittingbourne who died in 1704: included in his inventory were two lots of ready-made mantuas, which were listed with large groups of mixed clothing and described as 'ordinary Mantuas' and 'Girles Mantuas'[8] respectively, so presumably there were at least two sizes in ready-made clothing for women. Salesmen were located in towns and did not travel like the majority of Petty Chapmen and obtained their ready-made clothing from tailors. Travelling Petty Chapmen did not carry ready-made clothing, only the cloth for clothes among other small items.

The construction of these early mantuas of the late seventeenth and early eighteenth centuries was quite simple. The seamstress /mantua maker were, after all, beginning to develop the art of dressmaking using their existing skills. There were no paper patterns so they probably relied upon creating the shape by draping the fabric on a person. This simple yet effective method required the minimum of cutting and shaping. As women had no tailoring expertise at this time, their knowledge of construction came from their experience with making simple T-shaped garments such as shirts and chemises and possibly the informal robe or nightgown mentioned earlier. There is a logic in assuming that these women employed their existing knowledge and skills based on their experience in making chemises and nightgowns, for the original cut and construction of their early attempts at dressmaking. But they also had to learn to work with costly patterned silks where matching the patterns required skill. François Alexandre de Garsault mentions this in his 1771 book *Descriptions des arts*

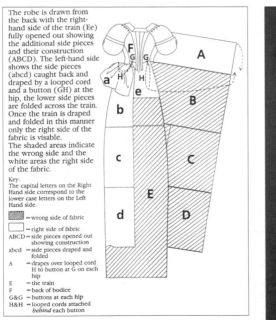

The robe is drawn from the back with the right-hand side of the train (Ee) fully opened out showing the additional side pieces and their construction (ABCD). The left-hand side shows the side pieces (abcd) caught back and draped by a looped cord and a button (GH) at the hip, the lower side pieces are folded across the train. Once the train is draped and folded in this manner only the right side of the fabric is visable.

The shaded areas indicate the wrong side and the white areas the right side of the fabric.

Key:
The capital letters on the Right Hand side correspond to the lower case letters on the Left Hand side.

▨ = wrong side of fabric

☐ = right side of fabric

ABCD = side pieces opened out showing construction

abcd = side pieces draped and folded

A = drapes over looped cord H to button at G on each hip

E = the train

F = back of bodice

G&G = buttons at each hip

H&H = looped cords attached *behind* each button

35 Proportional drawing of 1730s mantua

36 Back view of mantua opened out

et métiers: 'The greatest difficulty to be found when using fabrics with designs of flowers or divisions, is that of matching and arranging the material correctly while cutting as economically as possible. It is matter for genius and talent'.[9]

A surviving example of an early eighteenth-century mantua shows that it is cut from two lengths of silk about 20 inches or 51 cm wide, running from the front hem at floor level, over each shoulder to floor level again to form a short train at the back. The two widths of silk are joined along the centre back, the sleeves are not separate but cut in one with the width of the silk, where it overlaps each shoulder. A deep cuff with a short sleeve extension has been added to provide an elbow-length sleeve. The closely fitted bodice is shaped by broad single pleats running from the centre-front waist over each shoulder to the centre back to reveal a triangular section of the corset to be covered by a stomacher.

What distinguishes the mantua most from any other style of dress is the draped train. The front skirt panels of a mantua are constructed so that they can be draped at the hips. This was achieved by adding gusset-like triangular sections in the side seams to provide sufficient material for the train to drape properly over an elaborate petticoat worn under the trained mantua. Petticoats were often lavishly decorated with flounces of lace or silk and finished with a fringe at the hem.

By the 1730s and 1740s dressmaking techniques had become more sophisticated (figure 35, 'Proportional drawing of a 1730s mantua' and figure 36, back view of mantua opened out). The mantua bodice was cut with two front panels and shoulder seams, but with only one back panel using the full width of the fabric pleated to shape; the pleats were held in place by an inner linen lining. The train was constructed from a length of silk using the full width, selvedge to selvedge, forming a central panel which had triangular wings or gussets added on either side. This panel and the side pieces were attached so that the wrong side of the material appeared to face out, as seen in the shaded areas (BCDE) of figure 35. This was to facilitate the complicated draping of the train at the hips so that when correctly arranged, the right side of the fabric would be seen. The draping of the train had become formalised by the 1730s, and its construction altered. Instead of displaying the wrong side of the lining it became fashionable to show only the right side of the fabric when the train was draped and this showed the richly coloured and expensive silks to complete advantage. The drapery at the hips was supported on either side by a button and looped cord while the tail-end of the train was usually pinned up (figure 37). The successful pinning of the train and drapery arranged at the hips was not possible to achieve on one's own and could easily look unbalanced:

37   Back view of mantua and matching petticoat, 1733–34

Not Cynthia, when her mantua's pinn'd awry,
E'er felt such rage, resentment, and despair
As thou sad Virgin! for thy ravish'd hair.[10]

A helpful friend or servant was essential once the train or 'tail' as it was called, had been pinned and looped up it had to be plucked and tweaked into attractive folds, or as Swift put it, 'How naturally do you apply your hands to each other's lappets, ruffles and mantuas'.[11] Each of the buttons was stitched to the outside of the mantua towards the back of each hip, the looped cord was stitched to the inside immediately behind the button. The position of the button and the length of the loop were crucial to the final appearance. If the button was too low or too high, or the loop too long or too short, the whole effect was ruined, the Duchess of Queensbury wrote of her own mantua in 1734, 'I can assure you my tail makes a notable appearance'[12] (figure 37, back view of mantua and matching petticoat 1733–34).

Notes

1 Randle Holme, *The Academy of Armory and Blazon*, 1688, Book III, pp. 97, 98.

2 *Ibid.*, Book III, p. 94.

3 John Nevinson, quoted in *The Connoisseur*, 1955, vol. 136, p. 87.

4 Robert Latham and William Matthews (eds), *The Diary of Samuel Pepys*, 1666, London, Bell and Sons, 1972, p. 325.

5 Holme, *Academy of Armory*, p. 95.

6 *Ibid.*

7 Margaret Spufford, *The Great Reclothing of Rural England in the Seventeenth Century*, London, The Hambledon Press, 1984, p. 210.

8 *Ibid.*, p. 215.

9 Quoted by Janet Arnold in her book *Patterns of Fashion c. 1600–1860*, Basingstoke, Macmillan, 1985, p. 6.

10 Alexander Pope, *The Rape of the Lock*, Canto IV, 1–10, p. 106 in *Selected Poetry and Prose*, William Wimstatt (ed.), London, Holt Reinhart, 2nd edn, 1972.

11 Jonathan Swift, quoted in Dr Johnson's *Dictionary*, 1811.

12 *Letters of Henrietta Countess of Suffolk 1712–1767*, 2 vols, 1824, vol. 1, p. 68.

8 ✧ Muses and mythology: classical dress in British eighteenth-century female portraiture

Aileen Ribeiro

O NE of the great problems in any discussion of dress in portraiture is the difficulty of establishing studio practice with regard to the choice of costume in such works of art. We have little enough information about fashionable dress in the studio and hardly any about the role of 'classical' dress or draperies. Who, for example, set the agenda for such images: the artist or the sitter? What did the studio possess – if anything – in the form of clothing, draperies or pattern books? How much did the constraints of time and money promote the 'classical' look in women's portraiture, which could conveniently be allied to intellectual artistic trends?

Any answer must be mainly speculative, for it is hard to discern the authentic voice of female sitters apropos their painted images. It is probably true, however, that the clothing of classical antiquity was more admired by artists (and dress reformers) than by women themselves, particularly when it was contrasted with the perceived ills of high fashion. According to the *European Magazine* of 1785, for example, female fashion was dictated by 'caprice ... [and] desire of novelty', and it was only the Greeks and Romans who had 'freedom and ease' in their 'loose, simple and unconfining' clothing. Thus the artifice and transience of contemporary fashionable modes was set against the 'natural' lines of what were – erroneously – considered to be the simple drapes of antiquity.

In the context of portraiture, then, such a costume would be considered appropriate for women of intellect, such as writers and artists. A portrait by Francis Cotes in the 1760s (National Gallery of Victoria, Melbourne) which may depict the artist Mary Moser, shows a woman in 'antique' draperies; and in Richard Samuel's *Nine Living Muses of Great Britain* (figure 38) exhibited at the Royal Academy, 1779, most of the identified women of letters and arts wear equally vague 'classical' garb only partially related to the tunic and mantle of antiquity. Among the nine Muses (who are companions to Apollo – his statue occupies a plinth in front of the draped capitals) are the literary hostess Elizabeth Montagu (seated with her hand

38   Richard Samuel, *The Nine Living Muses of Great Britain*, *c.* 1779

to her chin, on the right) and next to her the historian Catherine Macaulay; next to her, and standing centre stage is the singer Elizabeth Sheridan, representing Terpsichore, the muse of lyric poetry and dance. The only 'muse' wearing something other than generalised classical dress is the artist Angelica Kauffman at her easel on the left; she wears oriental costume, the kind of fashionable *déshabillé* in which she often depicted her clients.

Compared to the situation in France, where there was a more highly developed sense of the classical past, and even publications on the costume of antiquity, in England there was less interest in this aspect of the arts of Greece and Rome, and a consequently less serious attitude, perhaps dwelling on the supposedly 'revealing' nature of this type of clothing. For example, it was as Iphigenia that Elizabeth Chudleigh went to a masquerade at Ranelagh in 1749, appearing – so excited reports said – in what might be the first topless dress. Elizabeth Montagu noted that Miss Chudleigh

39 Friedrich Rehberg, plate IV from *Lady Hamilton's Attitudes*, 1794

'as Iphigenia for the sacrifice, was so naked, that the High Priest might easily see the entrails of the victim'.[1] I suspect that in the context of what the eighteenth century perceived as 'indecent', she was probably not wearing stays under a transparent linen shift.

At the end of the century, another adventuress, Emma Hamilton (figure 39), inspired by the famous collection of Greek vases owned by Sir William Hamilton (and possibly also by images of the bacchantes in Cicero's villa at Pompeii), performed her famous 'Attitudes' or *tableaux vivants*; Lady Betty Foster described her as 'draped exactly like a Grecian statue' in a white chemise gown, and a 'sash in the antique manner'.[2] By this time, the neo-classical look was all the rage in fashionable circles, and Lady Betty herself with her dear friend the Duchess of Devonshire can be seen in a miniature of *c*.1791 (figure 40) in a pose from an antique vase, dressed *à l'antique* in tunic top over an under-dress, a style based on the Greek tunic called a *chiton*. At this point in the history of dress, aesthetic theory marches hand in hand with fashion; artistic convention merges into the reality of actual costume. When the artist Tischbein saw Lady Charlotte Campbell (figure 41) in Rome in 1789, he likened her to one of the 'swaying dancers of the paintings at Herculaneum',[3] and he shows her in a white dress, gauzy scarf and gold-embroidered silk shoes; the roses in

40   Jean-Urbain Guérin, *The Duchess of Devonshire and Lady Elizabeth Foster, c.* 1791

41   Johann Heinrich Wilhelm Tischbein, *Lady Charlotte Campbell, c.* 1789–90

her hair indicate that she may represent Erato, the muse of love poetry and song. A decade later, in 1803, the artist Robert Fagan painted himself and his wife (figure 42), and in this portrait, which must have been for private consumption, there is a curious and erotic contrast between his conventional blue cloth coat and starched linen, and the virtual nudity of the woman, a scarf binding her hair after the fashion of antiquity, and her white tunic only held up by the belt or *strophion* under her splendid bosom.

Representation of women in classical dress, whether for masque, masquerade or merely as a fashionable artistic convention, can be seen well before the eighteenth century as part of an international code of visual aesthetics. From the 1760s, however, under the aegis of the theories Joshua Reynolds was developing, of the virtues of 'timeless' costume in women's portraiture (by which he meant draped garments based on classical proto-types), it is possible to see a marked increase in the numbers of women in mythological guise.

Two fairly early portraits by Reynolds indicate this trend, and it is interesting to see the different ways of interpreting the antique. In a *c.* 1760 portrait (Lady Lever Art Gallery, Port Sunlight) Elizabeth Gunning, Duchess

42   Robert Fagan, *The Artist and his Wife*, 1803

of Hamilton and Argyll is portrayed as Venus with her doves; her arm rests upon a relief showing the *Judgement of Paris*, and she wears what was to become a staple of the Reynoldsian wardrobe, a white cross-over gown (or bed gown) girdled slightly above the natural waist. She leans on her peeress's ducal mantle, a gesture to her status in life. This mixture of the vaguely antique, in the shape of the white dress, and the contemporary, the red ermine-trimmed mantle, bears out what the artist was later to articulate in his *Seventh Discourse* of 1776, that women in portraiture should wear 'something of the general air of the antique for the sake of dignity, and … something of the modern for the sake of likeness'.[4]

It is in this same *Discourse* that Reynolds refers to Greece and Rome as the fountains from which all excellence flows, even with regard to their dress, and in his portrait of *Lady Sarah Bunbury Sacrificing to the Graces* of 1765 (figure 43), a much clearer debt to classical antiquity can be seen, even down to the classical décor; the whole is clearly influenced by the somewhat pedantic art of Joseph-Marie Vien. The Graces presided over the arts of civilised living, but it is clear that if Lady Sarah were to try to walk in her over-long trailing gown, she would quickly trip up – not very elegantly. The apt relationship of ancient to modern in terms of dress and

43   Sir Joshua Reynolds, *Lady Sarah Bunbury Sacrificing to the Graces*, 1765
44   George Romney, *Anne Verelst*, c. 1771–72

in the portrait as a whole, can sometimes be better achieved by artists less prone than Reynolds to academic theorising. For example, in Romney's 1771–72 portrait of Anne Verelst (figure 44), painted shortly after her marriage (she holds a rose in her hand), the fashionable hairstyle, along with a feel for actual fabrics, gives a sense of truth to what is essentially an invented costume, but a beautifully rendered blue silk gown over a white dress, with sash and shoes of matching sea-green. Close examination of Romney's portraits, and analysis of the clothing depicted in his portraits at the Huntington Library and Art Museum, convinces me that the artist must have had studio clothes of this kind, as distinct, for example, from the indeterminate draperies used by Reynolds. Anne Verelst's pose is taken from the statue of the Mattei Ceres in the Vatican, which Romney would have known from a cast or an engraving. His son, in his memoirs of his father, commented: 'He knew how to unite Grecian grace with Etruscan simplicity'.[5]

If we turn from the Muses and 'the general air of the antique' towards the personification of classical goddesses, we find that some roles were more popular than others. I use the word 'roles' deliberately, for there is often a sense of drama, even of a slightly tongue-in-cheek theatricality; women, denied a stage in the world of work of most professional occupations where uniforms and official clothing were *de rigueur*, and not entitled to wear the elaborate luxury of knightly orders, could inhabit, at least on the canvas if not in life, the fantasy world of mythology. It is interesting to see what is *not* popular in such portraiture; the stern and chaste goddess Minerva, for example, warlike and intellectual (and also patron of such crafts as spinning and weaving) figures as a character only at masquerades and in the theatre. The goddess Diana on the other hand, a young virgin, although she also presides over childbirth, and identified with the hunt and with forests, was to be seen as a popular choice for both masquerades and portraiture. A statue of Diana stood in Vauxhall Gardens, where masquerades took place, and in a 1772 Carrington Bowles engraving of 'Lady Betty Bustle', the caricaturist shows the costume worn at a masquerade in the Pantheon in Oxford Street. The fussy, three-dimensional theatricality of the costume, with its braid, fringe, ribbons and an *embarras de richesse* of fake jewellery contrasts with the gauzy simplicity of the greenish dress and red mantle decorated with gold, worn by Jane Maxwell, Duchess of Gordon (figure 45) in Angelica Kauffman's portrait of the same date. The only unifying factor here is the crescent moon in the hair, symbol of the goddess as divinity of light, although Cesare Ripa in his emblem book, *Iconologia* (1593) lists it as a symbol of inconstancy. Furthermore, if we read contemporary accounts of masquerades, it appears that the role of Diana was rather risqué, even improper; all I would add here is that when the future Madame de Pompadour met Louis XV for the first time in 1745, it was at a *bal masqué* at Versailles, and she came as Diana, perhaps on the hunt for something other than deer.

It seems at times that in an English context, antiquity could only flourish in terms of what the artist Lawrence called 'half history', portraits, that is, with some genuflexion towards classical dress and accessories, but firmly anchored to the social status of the sitter, as in Reynolds's *Lady Blake as Juno* (figure 46) of the mid-1760s, where the sitter is accompanied by a rather small and depressed peacock. Juno could be seen as the idealised type of wife, goddess of marriage and maternity, one of her symbolic attributes being a pomegranate, signifying fruitfulness and conjugal love, and thus an appropriate choice for portraiture of this kind; but against this we should remember Juno's cruel treatment of her rivals, such as Io, to which the Argos-eyed peacock bears witness. Furthermore, it has to be said that the private lives of many of these fashionable society figures –

45   Angelica Kauffman, *Jane Maxwell, Duchess of Gordon as Diana*, 1772

46   Sir Joshua Reynolds, *Lady Annabella Blake as Juno*

Reynolds's Lady Sarah Bunbury and Lady Blake, for example – were quite as convoluted as the sexual politics on Mount Olympus, so that the classical allusions very much pertained to the symbolic over and above the 'real'.

Finally, another popular classical figure was Hebe, goddess of youth, and cup-bearer at divine feasts; as the daughter of Jupiter she usually appears accompanied by one of the earthly forms assumed by her father, the eagle. Reynolds's *Mrs Musters as Hebe* (Kenwood House) exhibited at the Royal Academy in 1785, floats around in a wondrous confection of brown and cream draperies. Some twenty years later, when the fashion for the classical was at its height, Beechey painted Lady Burrell as Hebe (figure 47) in a white, short-sleeved dress *à la mode*, her hair dressed in contemporary 'antique' style. Again, although Hebe is the personification of domesticity, there are erotic possibilities in the menacing eagle, and, in Greek legend, Hebe was, through a mishap, accused of indecency, her place as cup-bearer being taken by Ganymede. This may explain why, for example, Gavin Hamilton painted Lady Hamilton as Hebe, bare-breasted *c.* 1786 (Stanford University Art Museum). Clearly, then, attitudes towards

47 Sir William Beechey, *Lady Burrell as Hebe*, 1804

48 Photograph by Henry Van der Weyde of *Sybil St Clair Erskine, Countess of Westmoreland, as Hebe* at the Devonshire House Ball, 1897

the representation of classical dress in female portraiture were more complex in the eighteenth century than thus might at first appear.

The popularity of classical deities continued to flourish during the following century, although more in life than in art, in dramatic guise rather than on canvas. In the eighteenth century, going to a masquerade as Juno or Hebe presented problems as to what to do with the accompanying birds. But at the famous Devonshire House Ball to celebrate Queen Victoria's Jubilee in 1897, one of the guests, the Countess of Westmoreland, found the solution when she came as Hebe – wear a stuffed eagle on your shoulder (figure 48).

Notes

This chapter originates from the 1995 Association of Art Historians Conference.

1 E. J. Climenson (ed.), *Elizabeth Montagu, the Queen of the Blue–Stockings*, London, 2 vols, 1906, vol 1, p. 264.

2 D. M. Stuart, *Dearest Bess: The Life and Times of Lady Elizabeth Foster, afterwards Duchess of Devonshire*, London, 1955, p. 59.

3 J. W. Tischbein, *Aus Meinem Leben*, quoted in S. Stevenson and H. Bennett (eds), *Van Dyck in Check Trousers*, Scottish National Portrait Gallery, Edinburgh, 1978, p. 37.

4 J. Reynolds, *Discourses on Art*, ed. R. Wark, New Haven and London, 1975, p. 140.

5 J. Romney, *Memoirs of the Life and Works of George Romney*, London, 1830, p. 162.

9 ✧ Dressing for art's sake: Gwen John, the Bon Marché and the spectacle of the woman artist in Paris

Alicia Foster

Gwen John spent most of her career as an artist living and working in Paris. From the turn of the century to the late 1910s, a period in which the French capital was perceived as the centre of the fashion world, the artist's letters discuss *la mode* and shopping for clothes, and dress also has a significant role in her paintings of women. Women's involvement in this aspect of modern urban life is of course generally accepted; what is more problematic is the interest of a woman artist in this area, specifically Gwen John, who is usually described as a solitary and self-neglecting figure who had no interest in such worldly matters as fashion and her appearance. Addressing the contradiction between this image of the artist and her own representation of clothes and shopping does not mean that Gwen John-as-recluse will be replaced by Gwen John-as-clothes-horse. The image of the retiring unworldly artist was, after all, *one* of the self-representations which she created. However the critical emphasis upon solitude and withdrawal as the central 'truth' of the artist's subjectivity will be brought into question.

The critical oversight of Gwen John's interest in shopping and fashion is informed by hierarchies of value within cultural criticism. Fashion is usually placed in the category of the lesser decorative arts within cultural discourse, and women during the late nineteenth and early twentieth centuries are often described as consumers rather than creators of *la mode*. As a result, femininity, perceived as consuming rather than making, has been defined as culturally insignificant and uncreative. In order for Gwen John to be constituted as an artist of value she has had to be represented as unlike other women, not involved in those activities and interests which have been designated 'feminine,' hence the critical significance given to her supposedly reclusive personality. The construct of the woman artist as recluse also functions to separate Gwen John and her work from what was undoubtedly a significant period and location in art history. Although she may be an admired artist, she is not placed in the same league as the important, and male, artists and movements of early twentieth-century Paris.

Such categorisations are clearly disrupted by Gwen John's self-representation in her letters as a woman artist involved in the activities of choosing and buying clothes and dressing up for Parisian life, and the significance given to women's dress in some of her art. This provides a different frame for her work, that of the politics of appearance in the French capital.

Paris, during the late nineteenth and early twentieth centuries, is represented in art history as one of the centres of the art world. At the turn of the century the city was heavily marketed as a centre of tourism and consumerism, a city of spectacle. Within these discourses the female inhabitant/spectator of the city has been positioned differently from the male. In art history she is often present as object of the male artist's gaze rather than cultural producer, and within guidebooks and souvenirs of Paris she usually figured as one of the sights. The spectacle of the French capital has been mediated through the figure of the male *flâneur*. There is now a body of feminist remappings of the city which has challenged the idea that women were merely part of the spectacle, and have debated the possibility of the female *flâneuse*.[1] What is at stake here is the perception of Paris in art history, and the possibility of moving a women artist like Gwen John, who lived and worked in the French capital, from a marginal space either cut off from public life or as one of the sights, to a central position as an active interpreter of the city and viewer of its spectacle.

At the turn of the century the French capital was home to large numbers of women artists from Europe and America, many of whom had come to Paris to work in its ateliers and remained to pursue careers as professional artists. Gwen John first visited Paris and studied in Whistler's Académie Carmen in the winter of 1898–99, sharing an apartment with two women friends who had trained with her at the Slade. She moved there permanently in 1904, settled in Montparnasse and became involved in its community of women artists. As well as being a long-established centre of art practice, the urban development of Montparnasse over this period was part of the continuing transformation of Paris into a city of spectacle. During the 1900s the boulevard Raspail was extended down to meet the place Denfert Rochereau, cutting a swathe through the networks of artists studios. Gwen John was also close to famous sites of leisure and consumerism, the Jardin du Luxembourg and the Bon Marché. Between 1904 and 1907 she lived directly opposite the Bon Marché at 7 rue St Placide, and from 1907 until 1909 she lived only one street away at 87 rue du Cherche-Midi.

Gwen John can be located at the heart of the city of spectacle, in which individual appearance had taken on a new significance. Social commentators of the early twentieth century addressed the conflation of appearance with identity in the modern city and created categories of urban types. In an article of 1903, 'The Metropolis and Mental life', Georg Simmel argued that modern inhabitants of the city needed to make themselves noticeable in the crowd in order to claim a position and a sense of their own identity in the 'swift and continuous shift of external and internal stimuli' which characterised city life.[2] Looking specifically at the role of fashion in the urban environment in an essay of 1904, Simmel argued that women in particular were tied to the world of fashion and its construction of visual identity through appearance, writing that 'it seems as though fashion were the valve through which woman's craving for some measure of conspicuousness and individual prominence finds vent, when satisfaction is denied her in other fields'.[3] Octave Uzanne's book *The Modern Parisienne* divided the female inhabitants of the French capital into different categories, including 'Artists and Bluestockings'.[4] Scathing about creative and intellectual women, Uzanne argued that the ideal feminine type was the Parisienne, who concerned herself solely with domesticity and adherence to *la mode*. The identity of the Parisienne was signalled by her slavish following of fashion, described in *The Modern Parisienne* as a hierarchy in which women obeyed the dictates of couturiers, 'Paris is the capital of fashion, and every day from its headquarters issue the decrees of the sovereign. Parisiennes are compelled to pose as models to the universe, and to reclothe themselves at the beginning of each season according to the caprice of her sumptuary laws'.[5] The construction of feminine identity through dress took place at the heart of the Parisian fashion industry itself. During the early twentieth century, the House of Worth gave each of its designs an individual name. A wealthy client could buy a 'Grisette' or 'Aviatrice' dress, and masquerade in clothes which suggested identities as diverse as Parisian left-bank bohemianism or the dashing modernity of a woman aeroplane pilot for different social occasions.[6] The fabrication of types of femininity through dress, which had become a feature of the fashion industry and social commentary, frames the creation of identity through costume by women artists in Paris, such as Gwen John. Dressing for city life could have great significance. Just as a particular style of dress could signal that a woman was a Parisienne, so her choice of clothes could also create and signal other identities.

Among Gwen John's papers is a handwritten list of clothes and their prices:

des souliers	11	25
une ceinture	7	45
un chapeau	19	75
robe nettoyé	4	00
des gants	2	75
	45	25
une ombrelle	6	50[7]

In comparison with the garments and accessories in Bon Marché catalogues, the items Gwen John listed were not the cheapest available, but from the middle price range at the shop.[8] In her letters, both those sent to the sculptor Auguste Rodin and signed 'Marie', and those addressed to women friends as 'Gwen', Gwen John wrote about fashion and of visits to the Bon Marché to buy clothes. It must be emphasised that Gwen John's correspondence is not being interpreted here as evidence of the truth of what she or her friends wore or bought, rather as representations of herself and other women wearing certain clothes and shopping at the Bon Marché.

The establishment of the Bon Marché signalled the emergence of a new form of retail, made possible by developments in industry and transport. It was the first of the *grands magasins* to be built in Paris, and the largest department store in the world before 1914.[9] During the 1900s the shop was marketed as a world created for women. In publicity material produced by the Bon Marché, the majority of consumers shown entering the store and in other images inside the Bon Marché galleries and on its staircases were female (figure 49).[10] In cultural representation also, the shop was represented as a feminine domain.[11] There has been considerable critical debate over the relation of femininity to the evolution and expansion of consumerism. Rachel Bowlby has argued that the *grands magasins* have often been interpreted as sites of the seduction of women and the commodification of femininity, the strategies used by retailers to tempt female customers having been mapped on to the existent paradigm of the seduction of women by men. However as she also indicates, alternative interpretations of the *grands magasins* are possible.[12] The Bon Marché stocked a vast array of merchandise for women to choose from, and also had a reading room, an art gallery and a buffet. As late in her career as the early 1930s, Gwen John used paper from the reading room of the right-bank Grand Magasins du Louvre to sketch on.[13] Part of the city of spectacle which insisted on the importance of appearance, the Bon Marché nevertheless gave women a space in which to socialise and the opportunity to construct their own visual identities from the variety of clothes, fabrics and accessories. Worth himself was reported as having found this threatening, saying 'I don't want women to invent for themselves, if they did I should lose half my trade'.[14]

Gwen John's letters to Rodin and to her women friends are similar in that both represent their author's interest in choosing and wearing particular clothes, emphasising the significance of appearance for women in the art world. In addition, both sets of letters represent women's clothes as not simply ready-made, rather women are written of as designing, making and decorating garments and accessories, inventing and putting together new looks. Gwen John wrote of buying decorated hats, ready-to-wear dresses,

49   Agenda, 1906, Bon Marché
50   *Chapeaux non garnis*, 1908

gloves, shawls, petticoats, parasols and hair ribbons, and also gave accounts of buying dress fabrics and decorations such as ostrich feathers and imitation flowers to trim the plain hats which were sold at the Bon Marché to be decorated at home (figure 50).[15] Writing about buying trimmings to decorate her clothes and hats herself does not mean that Gwen John was representing herself as poor. On the contrary, Anne Schirrmeister has described how all but the most wealthy women would renovate their wardrobes by adding new decorations.[16] Home dressmaking itself was on the rise during this period, facilitated by shops like the Bon Marché, by the dissemination of advice and paper patterns in women's magazines, and by the invention and development of the sewing machine.[17] As Stella Mary Newton has identified, by the end of the nineteenth century, home-made, rather than just home-decorated dress, was increasingly worn by the middle class in those circles with artistic aspirations, as a sign of their aesthetic taste.[18] In one of the letters which she signed 'Marie', Gwen John wrote of making a day dress which she sewed on a boat trip, and of trimming a hat for everyday wear.[19] The artist's correspondence with her women friends also represents women buying fabric for each other, and making and sending each other clothes.[20] In one such letter to Dorelia McNeill, Gwen John wrote, 'I am going to have some new dresses soon – perhaps I shall send some over to be run up with the machine. I think I shall have a cream one again. I cannot think of a new scheme – if it was not so dear I should have a check one in silk. Have you any thoughts on any new schemes?'[21]

There is however one feature of the representation of fashion in Gwen John's 'Marie' letters which distinguishes them from the way the subject is dealt with in her other correspondence: they construct a particular type of self-representation through a description of certain costumes and explanations of what these clothes signified. 'Marie' wrote that her intention was to appear *'artistique'* and of her pleasure at the compliments of other woman artists when she achieved this appearance, and specified that this was better than being thought merely *'à la mode'*. Within these letters an *artistique* look is defined as a careful mix of fashionable shop-bought clothes with garments designed or made by 'Marie' herself, in order to distinguish the wearer from being a slavish follower of *la mode*, yet signal at the same time that she was knowledgeable about fashion. In one such letter 'Marie' described her design for a long black velvet 'jackette' which was not fitted at the waist and so was different from modish garments. She specified that it was to be worn with a fashionable shop-bought hat, creating a subtle interplay between *la mode* and a more unusual and individual style.

Gwen John's knowledge of Parisian fashion is evident in her use of fashion terminology in her correspondence, and in the colour, cut and style of the clothes she mentions, which are identifiable as contemporary modes and variations of them. The long waistless coat was an anti-fashion version of the *jaquette* which was illustrated in 1906 in Mrs Eric Pritchard's regular feature on 'London and Paris Fashions' in the *Lady's Realm*.[22] Although the cut of the coat was not *à la mode*, according to Mrs Pritchard, velvet was the most fashionable of fabrics.[23] Similarly, the ostrich feathers and imitation flowers which feature in Gwen John's letters were among 'the favourite trimmings for headgear' listed in the *Lady's Realm* in 1906.[24] The colours of the fabrics and clothes which Gwen John wrote of were also very much in vogue, including a grey dress, a *'corsage de velours, rose sombre'*, dark, cerise-coloured material, and the checked silk she mentioned in her letter to Dorelia. Mrs Pritchard listed the fashions for 1906, *'Vieux rose*, pale rose – indeed pink of every shade is certainly worn … grey, particularly in the new silky crepon, will continue to be a very fashionable shade this season.'[25] The extent to which Gwen John was creating a specifically Parisian identity for herself is highlighted by another of Mrs Pritchard's pronouncements, 'Stripes and checks, let me tell you, are the fashion of the moment and of the future. English women wear stripes, but the French are always faithful to their checks'.[26]

However, as Georg Simmel theorised in 1904, in addition to performing the social function of including the individual in a certain social group – in Gwen John's 'Marie' letters that of *artistique* women – fashion also demarcated the individual from other groups. Gwen John was concerned with differentiating herself not only from the conventional follower of fashion, but also from other types of artistic dress. In her letters and paintings of the artist's model Fenella Lovell she constructed a particular type of artistic identity, that of the *bohemienne*. Although Gwen John worked as a model herself during the 1900s, she clearly distinguished between her self-image and Fenella's, and the demarcation was made through the representation of Fenella's clothes. Gwen John wrote that Fenella dressed as a *bohemienne* and wore sandals on her stockingless feet. This image of Fenella links her to the paintings of women made by Gwen John's brother,

51   Gwen John, *Girl with Bare Shoulders*, 1909–10

52   Lepape, *Les Choses de Paul Poiret*, Paris 1911

Augustus John. In his paintings of his wife, Ida Nettleship, and mistress, Dorelia McNeill, both women are often shown with bare feet wearing clothes based on gypsy costume. This type of dress was not merely a source of artistic inspiration, it signified a type of feminine identity which Gwen John rejected for her own self-representation. Jane Bilton's examination of Dorelia's Bohemian image suggests a possible motive for this rejection. Bilton identifies how the art world was sexually divided in Bohemian discourse, creativity being defined as a male attribute while women, in their picturesque clothes, served as accessories to, and symbols of, male genius.[27] Thus Ida and Dorelia, who had both studied art themselves, were relegated to roles as Augustus John's muses.

Gwen John's two paintings of Fenella, *Nude Girl* and *Girl with Bare Shoulders* can also be understood as images of *bohemienne* femininity, and at least one of them was exhibited in 1910 at the New English Art Club, where Augustus John regularly showed his paintings and drawings of women.[28] Fenella is represented as a modern Parisian version of Goya's *Maja Vestida* and *Maja Desnuda*.[29] The *majas* influenced the format of the two paintings which Gwen John made of Fenella nude and clothed in the same pose, although in Gwen John's paintings the seductive languor of the *maja*'s look is replaced with a direct gaze similar to that of the Parisian model in Manet's *Olympia*.[30] The costume worn by Fenella in *Girl with Bare Shoulders* plays a significant role in the creation of her *bohemienne* image, and this is also linked to the representation of women in both Goya and Manet's work (figure 51). There is a striking similarity between the style and decoration of Fenella's dress and the high-waisted white dress with sash and bow worn by the Duchess of Alba in one of her portraits by Goya.[31] The Duchess was represented as a scandalous figure in art history of the turn of the century and, it was understood at this time, also to have modelled for the *maja* paintings.[32] However Goya's Duchess wears an elegant long-sleeved dress with a red sash and bow, while Fenella's costume is plain and inexpensive, its fabric, short sleeves and dark trimmings indicating that it is actually a form of undress, a modern chemise. Representing a woman in her underclothes signified a disreputable identity, as in Manet's painting of Zola's courtesan, *Nana*, which was exhibited in Paris in 1904 and 1910, in which Nana is shown standing in her petticoats.[33] By the 1910s the fashionable Parisian figure had changed from Nana's voluptuous corseted S-bend to a slim empire-line, and the chemises on sale at the Bon Marché at this time were high-waisted and decorated with dark ribbons. This development was distinctively Parisian, made famous by the work of the designer Paul Poiret who had launched his hugely influential revival of the empire line during the late 1900s (figure 52). Painting Fenella in a downmarket *déshabillé* version of Parisian *haute couture*, with art historical references, Gwen John represented her as that modern version of the *maja*, a *bohemienne* artist's model.

Gwen John also wrote of other types of visual identity created by women artists in Paris. In her letters, she described women artists wearing masculine clothes, among them the Swiss painter Ottilie Roederstein, who, according to Gwen John, wore a man's shirt, jacket and fob-watch, and whom she referred to as 'l'homme-femme.'[34] From George Sand in the 1840s to Colette and Nathalie Barney during the 1900s, women of the Parisian world of art and letters cross-dressed. However, by the turn of the century, Havelock-Ellis and Krafft-Ebing had categorised a new social-sexual type, the mannish lesbian, whose sexuality was visibly signified through her dress and manner. As Esther Newton has argued, although dressing in masculine clothes was not the sole possibility for women claiming a lesbian identity during this period, some adopted this appearance as a strategy through which they could identify themselves and recognise each other.[35] The emphasis on public visibility is suggested by a particular form of cross-dressing adopted by women of the 1900s, which involved wearing men's jackets and shirts with skirts rather than trousers, signalling a form of femininity rather than a masculine disguise. Gwen John's letters represent Ottilie Roederstein wearing masculine clothes only on her upper body, and Michael Wilson has documented the lesbian groups of Montmartre wearing men's clothes with their skirts in order to 'claim and occupy public space'.[36] Conversely, Gwen John wrote of another woman artist who created a visual identity as a fashionable Parisienne. According to Gwen John, the Irish sculptor Nuala O'Donel dressed expensively in *décolleté* gowns of velvet and fur, and received her guests in a luxurious atelier decorated with Persian artefacts and liqueurs in silver decanters. Despite Gwen John's criticism of what she termed O'Donel's 'bourgeois' clothes and lifestyle, she wrote of dressing in her best clothes for social visits to Nuala O'Donel's atelier and being complimented on her appearance by the sculptor.

Looking at Gwen John's early painting *Interior with Figures* (figure 53) in the context of the artist's interest in dress and the politics of appearance offers an alternative to interpreting it simply as an autobiographical record. Although it was painted by Gwen John in 1898–99 during the artist's first visit to Paris with two friends who had studied with her at the Slade, Ida Nettleship and Gwen Salmond, and does indeed portray these two women, *Interior with Figures* is more than a portrait, constructing a particular relationship between fashion and femininity. The painting follows the format of Parisian fashion plates, which had been perceived by several artists and writers (famously Baudelaire) as symbolic of modern Parisian life. Gwen John is documented as having had an interest in fashion plates,

53   Gwen John, *Interior with Figures*, c.1898–99

and using them as a source for her art during her first stay in Paris. Her friend, Ida Nettleship, was involved in researching and buying plates of the early 1850s for her mother, the theatrical costumier, Ada Nettleship. Ida suggested Charpentier and Fasquelle's 1896 book *Un Siècle des modes*

54 Charpentier and Fasquelle, *Un Siècle des modes feminines 1794–1894*, Paris 1896

feminines as a possible source for her mother's work (figure 54), and wrote to her, 'We want to keep these prints I am sending to you, they are so pretty. The one of the two ladies only indoors is not dated I thought it looked about right ... Gwen S. and J. are painting me and we are all three painting Gwen John ... Gwen J. is copying one of those fair dames in the fashion plates ...'. [37]

The composition of two full-length female figures standing in a sparsely furnished room which Gwen John used in *Interior with Figures* was the standard template of fashion illustration of the mid-nineteenth century. However the painting disrupts the conventional representation of fashion and femininity in fundamental ways. Interiors in fashion illustration were often sketchily indicated, sometimes in monochrome with coloured figures and foreground, in order not to detract from the detailed depiction of clothes. Nevertheless, indications were given that these were wealthy and comfortable domestic rooms, they were usually decorated with chandeliers, flowers, gilded mirrors and ornaments. Although Gwen John's interior is sketched in and is spacious, there are no signs of domestic comfort, only signs of culture, a picture on the wall and a pile of books lying on a small table. The absence of any other furniture or decoration suggests the redefinition of domestic space as a work space by artists like these women, and also emphasises their cultural activity.

The dress of the two women also disrupts the conventions of fashion illustration. The function of the fashion plate was to sell new looks to a female audience, creating a coherent image of modernity, whereas the clothes represented in Gwen John's painting are not fashionable dress of the 1890s. Gwen Salmond, the figure on the left of the painting, is shown in a high-waisted dress with very full short sleeves. This type of aesthetic costume was created by women in the art world during the latter half of the nineteenth century to signify an artistic identity which was anti-fashion in its simplicity and that it did not involve corseting. By contrast, Ida Nettleship is represented in a costume of the 1850s, with a full flounced skirt and shawl, suggesting that Gwen John perhaps copied the illustration of a dress from a fashion plate and superimposed her friend's head. The contrast between the two styles of dress, and the fact that neither were actually fashions of the period, signals a refusal to conform to *la mode*. This is underlined by the faces of the two figures, which are clearly portraits of individuals rather than the replicated image of the current ideal of feminine beauty used in fashion illustration. *Interior with Figures* interrupts discourses in which femininity was represented as commodified by fashion and as a passive part of the spectacle, in place of a uniform style it represents women artists trying on different visual identities, dressing for art's sake.

Notes

1 For example, Rachel Bowlby, 'Walking, Women and Writing: Virginia Woolf as *flâneuse*', in I. Armstrong (ed.), *New Feminist Discourses*, London, Routledge, 1992.

2 G. Simmel, 'The Metropolis and Mental life', in D. Levine (ed.), *On Individuality and Social Forms*, Chicago, University of Chicago, [1903] 1971, pp. 324–39.

3 G. Simmel, 'Fashion', in Levine, *On Individuality* ([1904] 1971), p. 309.

4 O. Uzanne, *The Modern Parisienne*, London, Heinemann, [1894] 1912, pp. 125–43.

5 Uzanne, *Parisienne*, p. 23.

6 Interestingly, among Worth's designs are 'Lamballe', 'Marat' , and 'Charlotte Corday'. V. & A. Museum, Art and Design Archive.

7 Musée Rodin.

8 For example, the 1905 Bon Marché catalogue, *Exposition générale des nouveautés de la saison* carries illustrations and details of women's millinery, ranging in price from 6 fr. 90 to 35 fr., including an elaborate hat at 19 fr. 75 described as '*Chapeau paille riz fin, forme Louis XV, drapé tulle et ruban, piquets de boutons de roses en cache-peigne*'. Bon Marché archive.

9 See M. Miller, *The Bon Marché: Bourgeois Culture and the Department Store 1869–1920*, London, Allen & Unwin, 1981, for details of the establishment and development of the Bon Marché.

10 I am grateful to the Bon Marché for allowing me to work in their archive and to reproduce material for this chapter.

11 For example, see Zola's novel *Au bonheur des dames* (1883). The cover of the 1995 Oxford edition features a reproduction of a painting by Felix Valloton of 1898 titled *Le Bon Marché*, in which women shoppers are shown browsing near elaborate displays of sale goods.

12 R. Bowlby, *Just Looking: Consumer Culture in Dreiser, Gissing and Zola*, London, Methuen, 1985.

13 See C. Lloyd-Morgan, *Gwen John Papers at the National Library of Wales*, Aberystwyth, National Library of Wales, 1988, pp. 46–9.

14 E. A. Coleman, *The Opulent Era, Fashions of Worth, Doucet and Pignat*, London, Thames & Hudson, 1989.

15 Letters to Auguste Rodin, Musée Rodin. Letters to Ursula Tyrwhitt, National Library of Wales.

16 A. Schirrmeister, '*La Dernière Mode*: Berthe Morisot and Costume', in T. J Edelstein, (ed.), *Perspectives on Morisot*, New York, Hudson Hills Press, 1990, p. 114.

17 For example, Annie Swann's magazine *The Woman at Home* was aimed at educated middle-class women and covered such subjects as employment for women, lady photographers and 'famous bachelor women of today'. In addition, it featured fashion news and illustrations of the latest trends, and ran a service for readers to order paper patterns for the new modes.

18 S. M. Newton, *Health, Art and Reason: Dress Reformers of the 19th Century*, London, John Murray, 1974, p. 156.

19 Musée Rodin.

20 Correspondence between Ursula Tyrwhitt and Gwen John. Letters from Chloe Boughton-Leigh to Gwen John. National Library of Wales.

21 Letter from Gwen John to Dorelia McNeill, *c*. 1904–7. National Library of Wales.

22 E. Pritchard, 'London and Paris Fashions', the *Lady's Realm*, XX, 1906, p. 647.

23 E. Pritchard, 'London and Paris Fashions', the *Lady's Realm*, XVIII, 1905, p. 654.

24 Pritchard (1906), p. 237.

25 Pritchard (1906), p. 111.

26 Pritchard (1906), p. 647.

27 J. Bilton, 'Dorelia and Bohemia', BA thesis, University of Manchester, 1988.

28 *Nude Girl*, *c*. 1909–10. Oil on canvas, 44.5 × 28 cm, The Tate Gallery, London. *Girl with Bare Shoulders*, *c*. 1909–10. Oil on canvas, 43.5 × 26 cm, the Museum of Modern Art, New York.

29 *Maja Vestida*, *c*. 1800–05. Oil on canvas, 95 × 190 cm, The Prado, Madrid. *Maja Desnuda*, *c*. 1800–05. Oil on canvas, 97 × 190 cm, The Prado, Madrid.

30 *Olympia*, 1863. Oil on canvas, 130 × 190 cm, Musée d'Orsay, Paris. *Olympia* was moved to the Louvre in 1907.

31 *Portrait of Dona Maria del Pilar, Teresa Cayetana de Silva y Alvarez de Toledo 13th Duchess of Alba*, 1795. Oil on canvas, collection of the Duke of Alba, Madrid.

32 Goya was the subject of a major exhibition in Madrid in 1900. William Rothenstein, friend of Augustus John, had published a book on the artist in the same year, in which he asserted that the Duchess was the model for the *majas*.

33 *Nana*, 1877. Oil on canvas, 154 × 115 cm, Hamburg Art Gallery.

34 Letter of 1908 to Ursula Tyrwhitt, National Library of Wales. Letter to Auguste Rodin, Musée Rodin.

35 E. Newton, 'The Mythic Mannish Lesbian: Radclyffe Hall and the New Woman', *Signs*, 9, 1984.

36 M. Wilson, '*Sans les femmes, qu'est-ce qui nous resterait:* Gender and Transgression in Bohemian Montmartre', in J. Epstein and K. Straub (eds), *Bodyguards: The Cultural Politics of Gender Ambiguity*, London, Routledge, 1994.

37 Letter from Ida Nettleship to Ada Nettleship, 1898/9, National Library of Wales.

10 ✧ The aesthetics of absence: clothes without people in paintings

Juliet Ash

The typical striptease relationship demands that the ... '[performer]', who has offered the definitive spectacle of ... '[their]' possibilities of satisfaction, is absolutely not for consumption. (Umberto Eco, *Misreadings*)

As far back as cave paintings, clothed persons have been represented in art. This chapter, however, engages neither with the dressed nor with the undressed body. Rather, the subject is representations of clothes themselves, as a legitimate aesthetic subject in their own right, and 'absolutely not for consumption'. These clothes are not for wearing.

In contemporary works of art, clothes have usually represented either a language of commodification (when the works have often incorporated texts as well as garments) or, alternatively, the painting of clothes as emotional representations of the absence of the human form, the human body that once inhabited them. These latter paintings indicate in the presence of 'living' clothes the memories of previous lives: the notion of life in death in its widest sense.

In referring to the way in which language suggests memories, Hélène Cixous writes: 'We are the learned or ignorant caretakers of several memories'.[1] To look at paintings of clothes, whether in portraiture or as the sole subject of paintings, installations or sculpture, refers us also to 'several' memories of clothes: as they have previously been represented; as they appear to us in our lives; and as imbued with memories themselves as the meaning of the work.

Paintings and sculptures of clothes without people populate the history of art. In what follows I have been selective, omitting obvious examples such as Van Gogh's boots and Magritte's bowler hats. This is because I wanted to investigate works which represent the two genres of 'clothes without people' – clothes as commodities, and clothes as memories of the absent.

Clothes have always been part of the artist's perception of the presence and absence of people. In portraits, the 'real' person, who was once present, is now absent, and it is the portrait which remains, thus reminding the viewer of the previous presence of both sitter and artist. In a portrait, the way clothes are painted indicate the relative absence or presence and the feelings of the person whose portrait is being painted, as well as the feelings of the painter towards the person as subject. In Rembrandt's self-portrait with Saskia, for example, painted at the beginning of their marriage, the clothes the bridal couple wear are painted sumptuously and in detail, almost as celebrations of their new-found happiness. Later, in old age, clothes have almost disappeared in Rembrandt's self portraits, and instead the focus is on the expression on his face, on the poignant (lonely) presence of himself and his feelings.

The reverse is true of Goya's *Portrait of Marquesa de Pontejos*. In Goya's portraits his lack of interest in his sitters as individual human beings is conveyed by his detailed painting of the fabric of the clothes, the feeling of the transparency of the fabric rather than the feeling for the tense, blandly painted face of the Marquesa. It is almost as though Goya deliberately absented interest away from the person and made the clothes all too present in their fragility and absurdity.

However, since the advent of Pop Art, clothes have appeared in the absence of their wearers. This is not coincidental, since mass consumption was at the heart of the Pop Art celebration, and clothes, for example Claes Oldenberg's large *Blue Pants* (1962), could, on one level, be seen as equivalent to hamburgers, Coca-Cola cans, magazines and Hollywood stars as icons of economically expedient mass production and/or consumption. Oldenberg's objects/sculptures are also, however, imbued with subjective meaning and are not repeats or comments on the world of reproduction, as are Warhol's. Clothes, here, represent a form of life at the point at which the object's material existence symbolises both objective and subjective change and thus the contradictory nature of material objects. So the blue pants are non-functional, since they are sewn up at the bottoms and stuffed. They cannot be worn and yet they give the impression of being an ordinary pair of trousers, hung over a suspended beam. The belt hangs limply, a sign perhaps, since these trousers are so obviously menswear (in 1962 at least), of disempowered masculinity, and yet they are suspended in space and are therefore at a point where they take on a life of their own, balanced in a void. The wearer is absent and yet the trousers move on their swing, implying physical movement, and because they are stuffed they also imply containment of a human form.

The same could be said for Oldenberg's *Dresses Blowing in the Wind* (1961). These dresses were made for Oldenberg's Store, which was an actual store where he produced wares at the back and marketed them in the front. The dresses are made of hard plaster, but they take on human movement as the fabric hangs and is buffeted by nature. The contradiction contained in a hard material which nevertheless gives the impression of movement imbues the piece with a non-static life of its own. As Oldenberg writes in the *Catalogue for the Store* (1961):

> I am for an art that imitates the human, that is comic if necessary, or violent, or whatever is necessary. I am for an art that takes its form from the lines of life, that twists and extends impossibly and accumulates and spits and drips and is sweet and stupid as life itself.[2]

In 1979, Jim Dine painted huge panels of almost architectural robes indicating human presence through absence. The robes become the land-scape of Israel with its specific light and its contradictory politics. In *Bethlehem* (1979), there is a calm beauty about the robe with the sun illuminating a corner of the neckline, perhaps setting at the place where the body should/could emerge. There are religious implications in the halo of light[3] but above all the robe has soft folds, hangs loosely, comfortably containing the absent volume of a figure without the figure. The painting accepts clothes as appearances and yet indicates their contradictory nature in different lights or tensions of fabric.

In *Light Comes Upon the Old City* (1979), the robe is dark and scratchily painted, the folds on the sleeves do not hang loosely but describe tension. The light is more intense in the neckline and background, leaving more shade in the foreground. It illuminates more of the painting and yet under the bright surface there is a foreboding of conflict. The floating robes haunt the viewer in an intriguing, ghostly way. As with Oldenberg's work, they are and yet are not figures, merged and yet separate from their background. They are both fearful in their intimation of absence and yet sensuously vital in their painterly presence.

When we turn to look at contemporary art in the 1990s, it seems that the work of some artists has extended the concern found in the work of Oldenberg and Dine with 'life as clothes', while others have explored the subjective/objective meanings of clothes rather than their subjective ma-teriality.[3] Recent postmodernist pieces have taken up and extended the idea of the presentation of the garment as indicator of meanings in the absence of people. They constitute a critique of all that the fashionable world stands for in relation to our notions of identity, consumerism and our technologically determined society, and much contemporary art that has concerned itself with the representation of clothes has deliberately taken on Victor Burgin's notion of the 'representation of politics'.[4] By this is meant the way in which clothes become merely the representations of a greedy, shopaholic, consumerist society. The artists have turned away from what he and others have termed 'humanist presuppositions'.

While agreeing with Burgin that 'a form of visual art truly INVOLVED in the terms of THIS society ... must of necessity begin, as Brecht put it "not with the good old things, but with the bad new ones"',[5] I should like to suggest that paintings which reinstate human emotions as integral to the existence of material objects may well be political. After all, the separation between subjective and objective existence in our materialist culture could be seen as one of the 'bad new things' criticised within the paintings, sculptures, installations and photography which depict the sensuality of garments in the absence of the human figure, rather than their existence as commodities. This is in contradistinction to the 'bad new things' which are also repeatedly integral to postmodernist art practice. These obviously 'bad new things' might include the more visible aspects of late twentieth-century society, such as the use to which technology is sometimes put, consumerism to the detriment of production, an increase in the manipulation of the mass media and popular culture by those in power, and attempt to stifle dissent of any kind.

Clothes speak a universal sentient language since they are for and of us as human beings across class, gender, racial and national boundaries. Even if people are dispossessed of all other *things*, they usually have some form of clothing to wear. Thus, some contemporary art has clothes as its subject, which is political in its ability to allow us to see clothes and our lives as aesthetic experiences; to perceive the possibility of our emotions in relation to people in their presence and absence; this is in contrast to an art practice that represents clothes as signs of our more sociopolitical existence.

Steve Willats's 1992 exhibition at the Institute of Contemporary Art in London, 1992, Multiple Clothing (figure 55) was a reminder of Eric Gombrich's words concerning language and visual representation:

> language can specify, images cannot. It is an observation which stands in curious contrast to the fact that images are concrete, vivid and inexhaustibly rich in sensory qualities, while language is abstract and purely conventional.[6]

Willats's pieces were ironic but also disdained clothes, since clothes were presented as little more than part of the communication of the commodification of things, or, as Jean Baudrillard says: 'In contradistinction to language, which aims at communication, fashion plays at it, turning it into a goal-less state of a signification without a message'.[7]

In the Willats exhibition, diagrams of the thought processes led to the 'works' and were interspersed with PVC 'shifts' divided into primary-coloured squares, or just plain black and white. The garments were two-dimensional canvases for the interplay of identities worn by the wearer of the garments. The first series of garments had been provided with

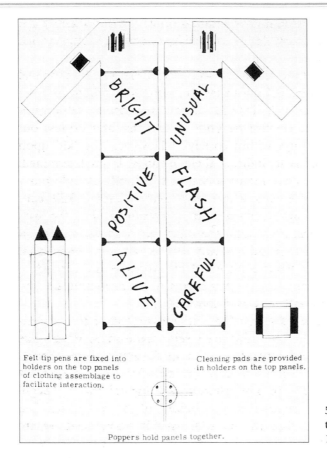

Felt tip pens are fixed into holders on the top panels of clothing assemblage to facilitate interaction.

Cleaning pads are provided in holders on the top panels.

Poppers hold panels together.

55 Steve Willats's exhibition, Multiple Clothing, 1992, ICA

labelled identities, written by Steve Willats into squares on the garments. In the next series, felt-tip pens were placed appropriately in pockets for the spectator of the wearer, or the wearer her/himself to write labels indicating the person's identity in the squares on the garment.

In the exhibition catalogue Willats explains:

> A person can, therefore, make fresh decisions about what they want the texts to say about themselves at any time, to reflect new feelings; furthermore they can change the assemblage from a jacket to a coat or a dress to fulfil different functions. Any choice and combination of texts is *permissible* and valid within the framework of each design, the only evaluations and responses coming from the wearer's changing relationship with other people. [my emphasis] [8]

Yet these garments were not designed as clothes, since they are two dimensional. Moreover, they are interesting only in so far as they pose questions as texts and not as image, about the individual in relation to society. They also tend to deny a history of dress which has already acknowledged that an individual's communication of a group identity can be communicated by the 'assemblages'[9] created by dissenting groups, which then become 'street style'.

Willats's piece, by contrast, seems to focus exclusively on the individual as perpetrator of their individual self-image as it relates to others, in order to celebrate 'personal creativity', since he states: 'This idea of self-organisation is equated with the creative freedom to organise and express our personal identity and feelings within society'.[10] However, the 'kit' upon whose surface the wearer is to indicate their 'feelings' is predetermined; and in his critique of our consumerist society – which allows little room for individual self-perception and where intercommunicative skills connected to emotions are impoverished – it is presumed that the 'kit', constituted as a text, or texts, will fulfil the individual's needs, in spite of the fact that it lacks both design and creativity. This is, of course, intentional and intended as ironic. Oldenberg marketed his works as art, expressing something more than commodity. Willats seems to be marketing his 'kit' as an ironic idea, but nevertheless as a commodity.

In order to rebel against society's (or is it governments'?) conventions and codes, in order to state the individual's self-organisation, Willats has produced an interesting and contradictory gimmick, where clothes themselves are denied validity. The piece begs the question of who or what controls the presentation and/or production of the original 'kit', if 'design' and 'creativity' have been banished in the making of the piece itself. We are told, in the catalogue, that 'the material used is plastic' and we are told why. The fact that felt-tips can be used on the plastic is merely an idea in relation to social identity, and the exhibits just ideas substantiated by texts.

This visual representation of clothes as signifiers of our 'identity' is oversimplified and cannot hope to indicate the complexity of late twentieth-century political and cultural identity. The work becomes a truism. The meaning of the piece seems to be that 'we are what we appear to be to others'. Thirty years after the sociologist Howard Becker[11] had developed 'labelling theory', Willats's work seems little more than a restatement of Becker's ideas. Becker coined the term 'labelling theory' to explain how deviants became categorised as such: they underwent a process of social labelling. Even at the time sociologists and criminologists criticised this theory for its oversimplifications, arguing that 'deviancy' was the result rather of a complex political class system than simply an almost fortuitous process of being branded as criminal. Not only had Willats's work not moved on from that position, in fact it may have been less sophisticated in its application than the sociological work that developed from the critique of Becker.

Willats's idea of the meaning of clothes appears one dimensional. Language and image are used in tandem in order to direct the viewer to a specific idea. Visual imagery is at the command of verbal language. The idea is predetermined and there seems to be little space for conjecture or feeling as to the nature of the absence of human form in the clothes represented. Clothes are a prop for the message and are used to demonstrate a prosaic argument similar to that of Alison Lurie in *The Language of Clothes*.[12] She perceives dress in psychological terms, as an extension of our personalities. We are what we wear or what we assemble ourselves or as and how we are seen by others. But what sense or memory of the wearer, over and above their stipulated 'personality', do we receive from garments in the absence of their wearer?

I want now to turn to a rather different exhibit, Marie Rose Cefai's Shirts, shown at the Whitechapel Open Exhibition in 1994. She used language less categorically, allowing the viewer to surmise the meaning in connection with the image. The components of the piece were: 'hair embroidery, white shirts, plastic packaging, stand'. Three identical shirts were laid out on the stand, representing, in their plastic packaging, mass-produced masculinity. In this piece too is found a critique of the lack of individuality in a society dominated by mass consumption, and of a flooding of the market with a conventional masculine uniform, which also implies a lack of choice for women as to what kind of masculinity they choose to 'consume' – or relate to, when besuited conventionality still triumphs over the more flamboyant images of the new man in the 1990s. The link between the image and the language of packaging is the concept of male power, embodied in the conventional men's shirts, which equate with 'the City'/Wall Street and/or political leaders. There are thus layers of meaning in a piece which evokes many possible readings in presenting us with the garment as a postmodern critique of the culture in which we live. Yet, as with Steve Willats's piece, there is no sense of the absence of people wearing the garments in their real absence from the work. Clothes are again seen as indicators of a critique of some of the more abstracted aspects of society, rather than as indicators of people, unless the absent men behind the shirts are considered as individuals and not merely as mass males, which I doubt. In this piece it is the presentation of the presence of the garments which becomes the implied critique through the use of them and not their representation.

In Christian Boltanski's installation, The Reserves – An Ongoing Clothes Installation (exhibited in 1988), on the other hand, used clothing was strewn throughout a vast room, like a jumble sale on the floor (figure 56). People were asked if they would like to walk into the room, 'to take in the smell, the vestiges of a human presence, now vacated'.[13] Some

56 Steven Boltanski, *The Reserves – An Ongoing Clothes Installation*, 1988,
from *Tate – The Art Magazine*, 1994

viewers did, but most strikingly – and Watson omits to mention this –
children refused. In the words of one child: 'It would be like walking on
people'.

As in the Marie Rose Cefai piece, real clothes are used to denote the
absence of people. In Boltanski's installation, it is the absence of holocaust
victims. But their presence is, to children at least, commensurate with the
people who wore them. They have been discarded, but still bear the traces
of their human wearers, and the clothes have thus, in our imagination,
become the people who inhabited them. It is the sense and memory of
the absent people which Boltanski has captured, without language directing
the viewer's thoughts about the subject; and it is our memory of people
who left these clothes behind which makes us sad and unable to walk on
them:

> Our own subjective singularities are in truth composed, on the one hand,
> of many other near or distant humans, we are carriers of previous gener-
> ations, we are, without knowing it, heirs, caretakers, witnesses of known or
> unknown ancestors.[14]

Some of the arrangements of clothes almost take on the shape of a
body, as in the dark mass on the right of the room. The clothes represent
dematerialised presence, and thus the previous presence and present absence

of people. The installation is both positive and negative in this assertion, since there is also aesthetic pleasure as the eye is drawn into the further corners of the room, where garments lose their edges and mingle into a mass of shapes and a variety of discarded colours and textures, reminding the viewer of the multiplicity of tastes and the possible pleasures people had from their clothing. There are thus contradictory feelings on leaving the installation: feelings of sadness at the absence of people; feelings for the abandonment of the people themselves as their discarded clothes, yet a simultaneous enjoyment in the clothes themselves arrayed together; also a sense of the memory of pleasure the wearers might have had in these clothes. The Boltanski installation reminded the viewer, by the presence of clothes, of the feeling of the previous presence of people in their absence. It was the emotional response which informed the particular political meaning of the piece.

Fashion photography, particularly as used in advertisements, has often used the absence of the wearer 'as a promotional message' [15] to indicate how dress can be part of and separate from a landscape. One example of this is an advertisement for a Fred Perry piqué polo shirt from the spring/summer 1994 range, where human absence/presence becomes insignificant in comparison to dress as part of the landscape composition of the backdrop. The shirt here, unlike the Marie Rose Cefai piece, takes on an austere presence of its own; colour and shape are part of, yet different from, its natural surroundings. The shirt is part of and distinct from the unpeopled landscape. The mood of leisurewear and the identification of the presence of colour in the landscape composition may be all the photograph is about.

By contrast, a Sarah Moon black-and-white Vogue fashion photograph of 1983 represents a dress which becomes the fabric of the wearer. A translucent dress hangs in an empty room by a window. There is deliberate confusion in the imagery as to whether there is a person looking out of the window. This is not just due to the blurring of the photograph, but also because the dress gives the impression of volume, of being inhabited, and is placed with the light coming in through the window behind it. We can imagine the transparent feel of the fabric, the patterning of the dress, from the intricate ironwork of the balcony. But we can also perceive the possible presence of the wearer in her absence and in so doing imagine how the dress looks when worn. The presence, though fragile, of the garment indicates both how it is and how the absent wearer was previously, or could be when wearing it.

Finally, the work of Colin Smith, in particular, examines the absence and presence of the human figure through the painting of clothes. His *Wardrobe* paintings are imbued with the haunting nature of clothes in the absence of people. The clothes in these paintings float unattached in space, as in Sarah Moon's photograph, and yet are given characters through the colour and quality of the paint, as in Jim Dine's *Robe* paintings.

Colin Smith is a contemporary of Marie Rose Cefai and Steve Willats and has exhibited widely, both in Britain and internationally; however, it was through looking at his paintings in his studio in the East End of London that I became acquainted with the vast array of these paintings of clothes. In his *White Shirt* (figure 57) for example, the subject is a shirt, but unlike Cefai's shirts in packages, it is genderless and has no hanger. It is a floating shirt, painted on an abstract background. The way it is painted describes the absent torso. It has volume. In the folds and shadows of the shirt there is the absence of the wearer, as in Oldenberg's dresses. Perhaps the subject of the painting is less the shirt than the absent wearer. For there is a human subject, despite the shirt being part of the background, floating in the background, unlike the Fred Perry shirt which, on its hanger, is a hanging shirt and distinct from as well as part of the background landscape. The shirt here, painted, becomes almost a portrait of the absent body. The shirt sleeves enfold space, the bottom edge of the shirt has a distinctive end to it, defined apart from the background, and yet if you were to take a small square of the bottom edge with a slash of the purple background, it could be merely shadowy white paint against the purple. There is a narrative here which verges on the abstract. A person is denoted by their painted spatial absence but the character of the paint suggests a breaching of the polarities of narrative and abstraction. The painting is not tied to a preconceived structure, nor does it define clothes as representations of messages. The variation of brush strokes describes folds, shadows in the fabric; the way fabric hangs and where 'the shirt' becomes more than just a 'shirt' or what it signifies, but where it becomes the 'feeling' of a shirt. The viewer can then be arrested by the point at which the shirt becomes more than a shirt, the point at which the shirt becomes abstract, part of the landscape, yet retains the haunting absence of a human form, precisely in the way it is painted. When the shirt is worn, however (see figure 58, left-hand painting), it again becomes a shirt, gendered, with a narrative. The subject is no longer the shirt, nor the absence of the wearer, but the man, albeit an anonymous, faceless, alienated man, with his bag and his shadow; the man with a purpose, in front of a warehouse door. The shirt almost retains less volume, when worn. There is no space in the shirt when inhabited by a body, and similarly it retains less space for the viewer's sense of the shirt as shirt and not as shirt, but as something else which suggests shirt and thus suggests the absence of the wearer, whoever that might be in the viewer's imagination.

Later, Colin Smith painted a series of huge, middle-sized and small

57   Colin Smith, *Shirt Study*, 1990–96

58   Colin Smith, *Night Train*, 1990–96 (left)
and *Wardrobe Series*, 1990–95 (right)

oil paintings on canvas or paper. The paintings represent wardrobes of clothes as landscapes of fabrics. They are bus queues of absent people, defined by and of clothes, hangerless but framed by the surface of wardrobes and suffused by light. Unlike the isolated shirt, and the figure wearing the shirt, the clothes are crowded together, intimate. These clothes in the 1992 Wardrobe series (see figure 58, right-hand painting) have volume, as though containing absent beings and yet they are but slashes of colour, slanting across each other; a variegated mass of texture, patterns and folds which fall out of the frame and yet are contained by it (despite the fact that the figures are mono, it is important that the colour in these paintings is discussed). It is as though a sleeve is there, shadowed, three dimensional and yet what is interesting is the way the fold line gashes what would otherwise be just a red surface, as the orange brushstroke to its left, and yet it also falls into shadow at the bottom. The clothes take on a life of their own, and the exuberant brush strokes emphasise this life, interweaving, overlapping each other; patterns merging and yet distinctive; the slanting light across the painting picking up on the sheen of the maroon garment to the left, and the bright-blue fabric, partly covered by the intricately slashed brown.

These are androgynous garments, painted as an intricate landscape composition rather than just clothes, and are peopled by the feelings of the absent wearers. In another canvas (figure 59) the white shirt is noticeable, squashed between a patterned garment and a blue tunic. It is crumpled now, as it hangs; its shadows and folds become it. Approaching the bottom left-hand corner there is a purple/white gash of paint. If we isolate this square of paint with the textured red on the left and yellow on the right, we can see an abstract painting, a landscape beyond patterning. The narrative has been eclipsed.

As Picasso once said: 'the interesting point is that which starts to become abstract';[16] and yet in these paintings the objects, the garments, remain, enclosing the human form, reminding the viewer of the absence of the wearers, as in the Boltanski installation. Here, though, the garments, as paint also, deliberately merge into abstraction; not the abstraction of coloured garment next to coloured garment, but as painted composition. The abstract quality of the paint, close up, allows the viewer to feel positively the texture, the vibrant colours and combinations of shadows and folds and as one moves away there is the feeling, the sense of the absence of the person, whose garments these then become. The haunting quality of the clothes is partly to do with the normally private nature of wardrobes of clothes. There is an intimacy about the way the clothes hang, almost hugging each other, and we, the viewers, are voyeurs as we look into a person's private domain, without their knowing. Yet in the presence

59   Colin Smith, *Wardrobe Series*, 1990–95

of these clothes, which contain the volume of the person as though they were inhabited, it is perhaps we who are being looked at by the more knowing clothes.

There are blue wardrobes and slatted wardrobes. In the first, the garments stand out from the frame; in the second, the frame seems to contain the garments. In one painting the light slants dazzlingly across the painting, across the fabric, across the folds; a shaft of sunshine across a field of colour. In another there are petticoats that peep out from under dashes of green and blue, and in the middle a layered white/red slash, shadowed at the top by the plain folds of a beige jacket, perhaps. There is a sense of the feel of the clothes uninhabited, floating, as they are, and thus the viewer receives intimations of the positive absence of the person in the almost human presence of the clothes. And yet there is also sadness in the sense of absence.

There is almost an exuberance about these clothes, standing proudly in the sun, not crumpled in the shade. The clothes take on the presence of the absent person. But there is a sense of loss, of death in life, combined with a celebration of life through the way the clothes are painted or constructed, as with Oldenberg and Dine. We take with us, as we leave our contemplation of these paintings, a positive affirmation of the previous presence of people. There are negative and positive feelings for these unpeopled clothes, as they anonymously float in their wardrobed frame.

Having looked at exhibitions, and at individual pieces within exhibitions, whose subjects in one way or another were to do with clothes, it was the explicit 'facture' or painterliness of Colin Smith's paintings which enabled me to perceive clothes as more than merely a sign: as both negative and positive celebrations of those who had at one time inhabited them. These were themselves a sensuous confirmation of human existence.

There was still a sadness at the absence, and yet the presence of the clothes could be positive in the memory they held of previous human presences. It had been the paintings whose narrrative had bordered on abstraction, without messages, without verbal language which had inspired the ability to entertain any positive memory of absence.

The absence of people, represented by uninhabited dress, is pervasive in contemporary art practice as a critique of consumption and of our consumption of identity. But we are often bereft of representations of the 'aura' of real human beings through their virtual absence as implied by the dress exhibited. When dress, as in Colin Smith's paintings, reminds us of a previous presence, through intimations of human form and colour, and allows our feelings as well as thoughts to ramble with our gaze, we may be left with a new perception of the world around us, an indication of a sensual awareness of the possibilities of change within the living of our material culture as much as an all too pervasive understanding of material culture. Colin Smith's paintings: 'are indeed floating signifiers, acknowledging that attempts to make reference to a "real" body of meaning are futile. These are not clothes that have never been worn, the folds and creases suggest fairly recent occupancy, yet they hover in the painted space, objects that cannot be assimilated or rejected, caught in the perpetual dynamic of desire'.[17]

Notes

1   Hélène Cixous, *Hélène Cixous Reader*, Susan Sellers (ed.), London, Routledge, 1994 'Preface', p. xxi.

2   Claes Oldenberg in Ellen H. Johnson (ed.), *Penguin New Art*, Harmondsworth, Penguin, 1971, p. 17.

3   Debates about the object in art practice have raged among artists and art critics in the late 1990s. For further reading on this subject, see Felicity Allen, 'Framing the Object', *Engage* (Magazine of the National Association for Gallery Education), 3, Autumn 1997, p. 43.

4   Victor Burgin, 'The Absence of Presence', in Victor Burgin, *The End of Art Theory*, London, Macmillan, 1986, p. 39.

5   *Ibid.*, p. 37.

6   Eric Gombrich, 'Image and Word in Twentieth Century Art', in Eric Gombrich, *Topics of Our Time*, London, Phaidon Press, 1991, p. 167.

7   Jean Baudrillard, *Symbolic Exchange and Death*, London, Sage, 1993, p. 94.

8   Steve Willats, *Catalogue*, Multiple Clothing, London, ICA, 1992, p. 1.

9   See Dick Hebdige, *Subculture: The Meaning of Style*, London, Methuen, 1979, whose term this is.

10 Willats, *Catalogue*.

11 See Howard Becker, *Outsiders: Studies in the Sociology of Deviance*, London, Macmillan, 1963.

12 Alison Lurie, *The Language of Clothes*, London, Heinemann, 1981.

13 Sarah Watson, 'The Life and Deaths of Christian Boltanski', *The Tate Art Magazine*, 3, Summer 1994, p. 38.

14 Cixous, *Reader*, p. xx.

15 Jean Baudrillard, *The System of Objects*, London, Verso, 1996, p. 164.

16 Quoted by Colin Smith in conversation, April 1994.

17 Alex Warwick, 'The Rim and the Abject', in Alex Warwick, *Fashioning the Frame*, Oxford, Berg, forthcoming.

11 ✧ Invisible men: gay men's dress in Britain, 1950–70

Shaun Cole

THIS chapter developed out of research I initially began for the lesbian and gay styles section of the Streetstyle exhibition held at the Victoria and Albert Museum in 1994–45. The lack of written information on the clothes that gay men have worn in the twentieth century led me to conduct a number of interviews with gay men about their clothing choices. In her essay 'Telling Tales', published in the *Radical History Review 62*, Elizabeth Lapovsky Kennedy highlights the importance of oral records in the recording of lesbian and gay histories, stating that:

> most social historians have transcended the polarization between the relia-
> bility of social facts derived from written sources – letters, newspaper
> accounts, court records – and from oral sources. They have come to under-
> stand that many newspaper accounts are based on interviews and
> recollections, and that letters are first person accounts. Furthermore, post-
> modern thinking has questioned the objectivity of historical accounts,
> revealing the partiality of all sources.

Following these caveats, this is by no means a comprehensive history of gay men's dress in the 1950s and 1960s, but represents initial findings based on the oral history work I have undertaken and experiences revealed in the small but extremely valuable number of printed oral history sources available, such as the Brighton Ourstory Project's *Daring Hearts*.

For most gay men, the 1950s were characterised by the very real fear of exposure, blackmail and arrest. The police were conducting a virtual witch-hunt of gay men, exemplified by cases such as the Montagu trials.[1] The legal position was such that dressing to announce one's sexual preference could lead to the loss of job or home, and could even lead to imprisonment. Therefore, most homosexual men followed the accepted dress rules of the day wearing 'dark suits, three pieces, very quiet shirts'.[2] To the majority of gay men it was important to remain invisible. Clothes were conventional and only small signals were given to indicate sexuality, for example the wearing of a pinkie (little finger) ring or suede shoes.[3] Dudley Cave remembers the clothes he was wearing when he met his partner Bernard in 1952: 'I was wearing grey flannels, a sports coat and an extremely butch belt, an ex-army belt, a tie. I wouldn't have dreamt of going into town in those days without wearing a tie and usually a sports jacket. Bernard was wearing a suit. Generally speaking we kept our heads down and tried to avoid being seen as what we were'.[4] John Hardy echoes the fact that everyday dress for most gay men followed conventions of fashion: as he says 'when you were out and about in the streets and going about your ordinary day to day business you wouldn't think of wearing anything really outrageous. You tended to dress down and look like everyone else'.[5]

One particular smart style of dress that was associated with middle-class gay men during the early 1950s was that of the New Edwardian. The New Edwardians favoured a tailored appearance that was in complete contrast to the popular American wide-boy look or the 'demob suit'. It drew heavily on the tailored forms of the period immediately following the First World War – overcoats based on army greatcoats, tapered trousers which finished just above the ankle and bowler hats, slightly too small, which sat forward on the head. This style of dress offered the gay men of the early 1950s a chance to be smart, while not quite conventional, maintaining a distinct sartorial edge over the average man in the street. The look was styled by

60 A group of young gay men wearing fashionable clothing of the day in the mid-1950s. There is nothing remarkable about the clothes or anything that indicates that these young men are gay

'a London minority consisting of ex-Guards officers and interior decorators, some of whom turned out to be both'.[6] While not all the New Edwardians were gay, the look was 'camp, that is to say it was equivocally witty and self mocking, but at the same time affectionate about what was being lightly mocked'.[7] John Hardy comments that the look was particularly favoured by:

> all the piss arrogant queens [who] used to go to The Rockingham and they all used to dress up in their three-piece pin-striped suits, starched collars and ... they all preened themselves and ... were all dressed a bit like Bunny Rogers ... [who] used to walk up and down Bond Street in this terribly arrogant sort of Edwardian fitted suit with waistcoat and lapels and a carnation or a rose in his buttonhole and chains and he always had a curly brimmed bowler sat on top of his head.[8]

In *Today There Are No Gentlemen*, Nik Cohn states that it was gay men who killed off the New Edwardian look as an ordinary middle-class fashion.[9] What this statement does not consider is that these gay men and the 'ordinary' middle-class 'Edwardians' could quite easily have been one and the same. Cohn does later point out that this style of dress lasted until 1954, by which time it had been taken up by the Teddy Boys and '*even* homosexuals were embarrassed to wear it' (my italics).[10]

On the whole, even casual dress in the 1950s was restrained – grey flannels, and a sports shirt with a tie or cravat and the ubiquitous suede shoes. It was in the suede shoes and socks that the signals were given – 'gaily coloured stockings – and when I mean "gaily" I mean just lisle diamond shape black and white. Your stockings could be a little bit outrageous. You'd stand out in the street, you were classed as "one of those"'.[11] The cravat was another item of clothing that added a slightly flamboyant edge to a homosexual's clothes, identifying him as such – 'the most dashing thing you could do at that time [1959] was to wear a cravat, an open necked shirt with a cravat in it. The nicest cravat I bought was from Liberty's'.[12] Michael Brown usually dressed in unremarkable clothing during the day, but at night when he was cruising (looking for sexual partners) at Notting Hill Gate he wore 'a plaid workman's shirt, denim jeans and a heavy leather belt with a large buckle'. This was, he asserts, 'way before the macho bit came into fashion'.[13] Another way for men to emphasise their homosexuality was to wear make-up with their conventional clothing. 'I did wear paint, make-up', says Daniel, 'I certainly wasn't a slut and I dressed ordinary. We had nice clothes, I mean it didn't mean to say that we had fancy clothes or feminine clothes. We looked feminine no way about it, but you dressed *nice*'.[14] It was in casual wear that changes in men's, and especially gay men's, dress were to be seen. As men were venturing into Europe, particularly Italy, on holiday, they were buying clothes and adopting a European style of dressing. The pressure to conform was removed in a foreign country and there was much less at stake in dressing in a non-conventional fashion. It was this influence that was to be found in the clothes made and sold by Bill Green at Vince Man's Shop.[15]

Vince was on the fringes of Soho where rents were cheap, next to the Marshall Street baths, a homosexual haunt where 'all the muscle boys and butch trade trained'.[16] Bill Green had started work as a male-physique photographer and many of his models trained at Marshall Street and bought the first clothes Green made. This was the shop's initial target audience but before long the clientele were not only 'Chelsea homosexuals' but 'a very wide public, within an age range of about twenty five to forty. They weren't teenagers, because teenagers couldn't meet our prices, but artists and theatricals, muscle boys and theatricals of every kind'.[17] Hardy says, 'by the cost of living, the prices of the time, they were quite expensive to buy. I mean a pair of jeans or a shirt would be about three guineas, which was about a working wage for a week at that time'. Hardy took a job as assistant at the shop and as part payment for his work was given clothes from the shop, which he felt offered the first 'really chic' alternative in men's clothing. Describing the clothes he both sold and wore he emphasises that 'if you look at those styles, the narrow jeans, say, and the skimpy shirts, that was more or less the Italian look'.[18] The clothes were undeniably camp but also fun, incorporating hipster pants, expensive tight sweaters and briefs. The colours of the clothes (bright reds, yellows and purples) were associated in the public mind with 'fairies' and 'queers', but it was not long before fashion-conscious young heterosexual men were making their way to Vince to buy their clothes.

The first clothes sold at Vince were extremely tight-fitting. Just as the New Edwardians had worn snugly tailored trousers and jackets, so Vince's clothing revealed the contours of the male body. Nik Cohn has referred to tightness in clothing being related very much to gay men.[19] This is echoed by Colin MacInnes in his seminal novel of 1950s youth culture, *Absolute Beginners*. His fashionable gay character, the Fabulous Hoplite 'was wearing a pair of skin-tight, rubber-glove thin, almost transparent cotton slacks, white nylon-stretch and black wafer-sole casuals, and a sort of maternity jacket, I can only call it coloured blue'.[20] It is extremely likely that this description is based upon MacInnes's knowledge of Vince's clothes.

Vince spawned a whole host of men's boutiques in and around the Carnaby Street area, which by the early 1960s was the fashionable centre of young London. Shops of this nature were not, however, exclusive to London. Brighton, which for a long time had been a Mecca for homosexuals,

61 John Hardy, wearing Vince jeans, and a friend in drag at the Hampstead Arts Ball, 1951

had its own gay-orientated boutique – Filk'n Casuals. The owners Phil and Ken had both been trained in Paris where Phil had worked for Worth. Harry, who maintained that Phil and Ken were making these clothes before Vince started, described the clothes as 'casual shirts, jackets, trousers and underbriefs, which were brief underbriefs like they wear them today, which were very daring in those days'.[21] James continued 'they were the first people to do beach shirts in gaudy jazzy Caribbean-type colours for gentlemen. Really, in those days, you wouldn't be seen dead in that sort of thing, you'd be thought to be *that* sort of person'.[22]

The Italian look that was made and sold by Vince, John Stephen and the copycat stores in Carnaby Street was taken up by the groups of fashion-conscious young men who came to be known as mods. It would be untrue to say that mod was an exclusively, or even predominantly, gay style. However, the clothes that the mods were wearing were those that gay men had been wearing for some time. 'The only other person we saw was a tall, well-dressed young Negro who bought a pair of the coloured denim hipster trousers. The Negro was obviously homosexual and I realized that homosexuals had been buying that stuff for years. They were the only people with the nerve to wear it, but in the early sixties the climate of opinion was changing, the Mods were wearing the more effeminate and colourful clothes of Carnaby Street'.[23] Tony was a teenager (well aware of

his sexual orientation) in the early 1960s and remembers: 'when I was in
the army [the fashionable look] was the Italian look, with three buttons,
that was very mod. Winklepickers that's what I used to wear. My trousers
were creased, my sleeves creased, everything: I mean I was going out like
a knife and fork'.[24]

Jon Savage, in his article 'Tainted Love: The Influence of Male Homosexuality and Sexual Divergence on Pop Music and Culture Since the War'
states that 'like the Edwardians, the mods assumed what had been an
exclusively and outrageously homosexual style and used it as a key to cross
into the "private" space of the body and of self-discovery'.[25] Peter Burton,
in his autobiography *Parallel Lives*,[26] makes comparisons between the mod's
clubs (the Scene) and the gay coffee bars (La Duce) of Soho, London.
Both groups were wearing the same clothes (bought at Vince and John
Stephen), listening to the same music (soul, ska, bluebeat and Motown)
and taking the same drugs (speed, known as blues or doobs). It is
impossible to say how much interaction went on between the two, but it
would be safe to say that some young gay men must have gone to the
Scene and, who knows, heterosexual mods may have wandered into La
Duce mistaking it for a mod coffee bar.

While many gay men were dressing in conventional styles to disguise
their sexuality and some were challenging conventions of acceptable men's
wear, while still maintaining some discretion about their sexual orientation,
there were others who refused to hide behind conventional clothing. Instead
of relying on small signifiers, their whole choice of dress announced what
sort of men they were. Some men, like Quentin Crisp, were deliberately
disobeying the accepted male dress codes of their day.[27] These obvious
homosexuals were often frowned upon by their more conventional
'brothers', as giving all homosexuals a bad name. 'Unfortunately, the
obvious type is the one we're typed with, you know. A lot of people
assume we're bitchy and effeminate and go around jangling bracelets, you
know, 'cause they're the obvious ones which normal people mostly see
and assume practically the whole homosexual world is like that.'[28] But for
some young gay men discovering that they were not the only one in the
world, dressing up was a means of identification, becoming part of a
recognisable group: 'When I really found out about this life, I was about
fourteen … I met somebody about my own age and they just took me
into town and then I went really effeminate. I let my hair grow long and
I dyed it, shaved my eyebrows off and put eye mascara on and all sorts
and I went really effeminate … and I thought marvellous … you know,
there's somebody else like me after all'.[29] While these men did not go so
far as to cross-dress in public, they accentuated feminine characteristics.
Their clothes were anything but masculine, as described by Grant: '[The

more outrageous] queens all wore terribly flared trousers and terribly Hawaiian shirts with all sorts of tulle at the neck. Hairdos were rather flamboyant, it was all out of a bottle. Handkerchiefs, kerchiefs round their neck for scarves ... they loved jewellery; they used to have not one bracelet but about *four* ... Colourwise it was a bit grotesque. Pink velvet trousers with a green shirt'.[30]

At private parties and clubs, men who normally exercised restraint in what they wore, could dress up in sexy, revealing clothes, flamboyant fancy-dress-style costumes or even in drag.[31] The Arts Balls held in Chelsea, Hampstead and Brighton were important events in the lives of gay men. John Hardy maintains that, although many of the people at these Balls were from the arts or were artists, the 'majority were gay'. Emphasising the importance of the Balls for homosexual men he continues that 'if the gay community in London heard that a Ball like this was going to happen then they would go and get tickets for it, because they knew they could be outrageous, dress in whatever [they] wanted'.[32] The open-minded, art-world environment allowed men to dress in whatever they chose and to dance together. Daniel, a gay man who dressed in fashionable clothes of the day describes the Arts Balls: 'In the late fifties, sixties, the theatres and arts always had a ball on Christmas. I went to several of them, actually, and of course it was very theatrical. They had a fashion parade. It gave you a chance to dress [up] outside, to drag up, yes. All the people that went there was good with their needles and the colours of the thing!'[33]

The Aquarium, the Brighton venue for these Balls, was known all over England. The importance of the Arts Ball at the Aquarium is highlighted by Grant who remembers 'a certain number of queens [who] used to spend the whole summer sitting on the Men's Beach [in Brighton] sewing sequins on the gowns ... by the hundredweight'.[34] At first the Aquarium turned a blind eye to drag, but for the last two or three years before it shut would not permit it. The Hampstead Ball too caused quite an uproar. A reporter from the local paper tried to interview some of the partygoers on the night bus provided to get back to the centre of London, but after being teased and sent up he wrote a scathing report about 'a lot of fairies at the Town Hall' and called for the Balls to be banned.[35] Drag and cross-dressing were not by any means confined to the Arts Balls. Other drag venues sprang up in London and Brighton, such as the 42 Club. Even as far afield as Bristol men were dragging-up during the 1950s and 1960s. Tony remembers that 'you used to get a lot of chaps [who] used to dress in drag and come to the pub in Victorian outfits. I had one friend who worked for a famous jeweller and he used to come out in Victorian fashion and it was perfect from head to toe and it was beautiful. It was a big thing for someone to do that, especially coming to a gay bar, dressed up like, until one got to the club'.[36]

Not all men wore feminine clothes to the Arts Balls. John Hardy wore jeans from Vince's and a brightly patterned bolero style shirt to the Hampstead Arts Ball in 1951. Some men took the opportunity to dress in 'butch' (or masculine) fantasy clothes such as army uniforms. A friend of John Hardy's 'went as an American sailor to the Vic Wells Ball at the Lyceum in the mid 1950s. That was one of the gay things at the time because sailor's rig at that time was quite sexy: white bell-bottoms, tight-fitting here around the waist and hips, tight-fitting cotton and the mess jacket and one of those little white cotton hats'.[37] These dress choices were more often than not limited to private spaces where gay men could be themselves.

In the 1960s, brighter colours became more prevalent in men's clothing. Eddie states that 'In the sixties, style started to change, people started to wear bright colours. If you wore a yellow sweater, it was considered very, very way out ... people were wearing red socks, that was the start of red socks'.[38] By the end of the decade it was far more acceptable for young (heterosexual) men to wear bright colours, effeminate clothes and even make-up. The age of unisex had dawned. In many ways the styles of dress previously worn by gay men unafraid of flaunting their sexuality had been hijacked by heterosexuals. However, dressiness and fashionable clothes were still asssociated with homosexuality in the public mind. A 1965 French guide to London recommended the Jaeger shop because its staff and clintele were not 'all homosexuals, as is almost always the case in boutiques for fashionable young men'.[39]

Fashion was still mainly conventional in provincial cities, despite having Chelsea-style boutiques. Dress choice for gay men depended very much on their occupation or place in society. Tony was living in Bristol and working as a window-dresser at The Button Hole, a boutique-style concession in Lewis's department store in the late 1960s. 'I would wear some very outrageous clothes because that was the era' he comments. 'I used to go out in [a] black lace shirt and say white trousers or black trousers, whatever went with black. I think that you would go out in those days but no one bothered you; they knew but no one bothered you in that respect.'[40] Tony's partner David was working as a chef in a factory and so his style of dress was far more restrained. 'Well, his going to work was very correct. I mean he'd dress totally down. No high heels, less exaggerated flares, no cravat.'[41] It is interesting to note that Tony felt that he was not harassed for being gay or wearing the clothes that he did, and yet his partner still felt the need to tone down his dress for work. As in the 1950s, gay men were still choosing to dress differently in public from

62   John Hardy wearing an American sailor uniform in the mid 1950s. This was the outfit worn
by his friend to The Vic Wells Ball

63   Tony on holiday in the late 1960s, wearing a yellow flowered shirt and flares

the way they did in their private spaces. It was still only in gay pubs and
clubs that men could really let themselves go in their choice of clothing.

In 1967, the Sexual Offences Act decriminalised sex between consenting
males over twenty-one in private.[42] Although this did not have immediate
effects it did begin to change the climate and public attitudes towards
homosexuality. The Stonewall riots in New York in 1969[43] led to the rapid
rise of gay liberation and demands for equality. Gay men visiting America
observed the growth of the gay rights movement and brought back both
the activist ideas and the styles of dress worn by the new generation of
'out' gay men. The clothes that these American gay men were wearing, the
gender-bending, androgynous clothes of radical drag and the ultra-macho
style known as 'the clone' were to have profound effects upon British gay
men's dress choices.

While not all gay men in the 1950s and 1960s were interested in what
clothes they wore, there was a significant number who went to great pains
to choose the 'correct' clothing to express their sexual orientation, often

only to others of their kind. Social, moral and legal restrictions led these men to subtly introduce codes and signals which could be built upon to create a visible identity or to flaunt their sexuality by deliberately challenging the hegemony of mainstream heterosexual men's fashion. In this chapter I have illustrated a number of the ways in which gay men achieved these aims and have shown the influence gay men's dress choices had upon mainstream (heterosexual) men's dress. Tony is adamant that: 'Gay style actually sets trends. It's what straight people take fashion from'.[44] The adoption of the New Edwardian and mod styles illustrate this point and we are left with the, sometimes grudgingly acknowledged, theory and fact that the dress choices of gay men play a vital role in forming patterns of taste in mainstream men's dress.

Biographical details of interviewees

Daniel was born in 1928 into a Roman Catholic family in Bermondsey, London. In 1939 his family moved to Carshalton in Surrey. He began his working life at Lines toy manufacturers in Merton and went on to become a nurse. Daniel has been heavily involved in work for London Friend and the Greater London Housing Association. He is now retired and spends his time running clubs for the elderly and working in the Liberal Democrat party.

Dudley Cave was born in Golders Green in 1921. He was called up into the army in 1941 and spent much of the war in a Japanese prisoner of war camp. After losing his job as a cinema manager around the time of the Montagu trials, he worked as a clerical officer in the hospital service. Dudley has been involved with gay switchboard since its founding in the early 1970s and set up the gay bereavement society with his partner Bernard Williams. Now retired, Dudley lives in London and is writing his autobiography.

John Hardy was born in 1931 in Sunderland. He worked as a farm labourer and was in the Merchant Navy before moving to London to join the Royal Horse Guards. In 1951 he got a job in Vince Man's Shop and undertook his first modelling assignment for the mail-order catalogue. John pursued a successful career as a model until 1972 and is now retired.

Michael Brown was born in London. He was a dental student in the 1950s and worked on Shaftesbury Avenue, London, as a dentist in the 1960s. Michael was an active member of the Gay Liberation Front in the early 1970s and has continued to have an involvement in gay issues and politics. He now lives in London and is engaged in research.

Tony was born in 1941. During the early 1960s he worked as a window-dresser in Bristol. This led to some modelling work in the late 1960s and early 1970s. In 1972 Tony moved to Benidorm where he ran a bar. He is now officially retired and living in the country where he makes masks and does some window-dressing on a freelance basis.

Notes

1 One of the most famous prosecutions of gay men in the 1950s. Lord Montagu was accused in 1953 of indecent assault on two Boy Scouts. The chief prosecution witnesses were offered immunity in exchange for reporting on other homosexuals which was a common practice at the time. The jury was unable to decide whether Montagu and his co-defendant Kenneth Hume were guilty. Before the retrial Michael Pitt-Rivers and Peter Wildeblood were arrested and accused of indecency and conspiracy with Montagu to commit the offences. A charge designed to jeopardise Montagu's retrial. After a display of malice and prejudice from the prosecution the defendants were found guilty. This case was typical of those brought against gay men in the 1950s.

2 K. Porter and J. Weeks, (eds), *Between the Acts: Lives of Homosexual Men 1885–1967*, 1992, London, Routledge, p. 62.

3 On a 1981 television programme *Sexual Identity*, Trevor Thomas, then in his late seventies, told his interviewer that he was known as 'the man who wore suede shoes'. Also quoted in Porter and Weeks, *Between the Acts*, p. 62.

4 Dudley Cave, interviewed by the author, 1997.

5 John Hardy, interviewed by the author, 1995.

6 Letter from Geoffrey Squire to the author.

7 *Ibid.*

8 Hardy, interviewed, 1995.

9 N. Cohn, *Today There are no Gentlemen: The Changes in Englishmen's Clothes Since the War*, London, Weidenfeld & Nicolson, 1971, p. 27.

10 *Ibid.*

11 Brighton Ourstory Project, *Daring Hearts: Lesbian and Gay Lives of 50s and 60s Brighton*, Brighton, Queenspark Books, 1992, p. 50.

12 Hardy, interviewed, 1995. Trevor Thomas, talking about his dress in the 1930s said 'I found out about Liberty silk ties and I wore those, but my big alibis [to anyone who was not gay] in all of this situation were (a) I was an artist, (b) I worked in a Museum and (c) I acted'. Quoted in Porter and Weeks, *Between the Acts*, p. 62.

13 Michael Brown, interviewed by the author, 1993. This was the look which was later to be popularised by gay men and known as the 'clone'. It has popularly been believed to have been imported from America with gay liberation. The fact that Michael Brown was wearing the styles and they were for sale at Vince's store in the early 1960s indicates that there was some attraction to these macho styles before liberation. Interviews with James Gardiner and Peter Burton confirm this theory.

14 Daniel, interviewed by the author, 1997.

15 For more on the influence of Vince's shop see S. Cole, 'Corsair Slacks and Bondi Bathers: Vince Man's Shop and the Beginnings of Carnaby Street Fashion', *Things*, 6, 1997, pp. 26–39.

16 Bill Green in Cohn, *Changes in Englishmen's Clothes*, p. 61.

17 Bill Green interviewed on BBC radio's 'Gear Street' as part of 'South East Special' series. Broadcast 22 August 1964.

18 Hardy, interviewed, 1995.

19 Cohn, *Changes in Englishmen's Clothes*.

20 C. MacInnes, *Absolute Beginners*, London, 1959, Allison and Busby, p. 51.

21 Brighton Ourstory Project, p. 53.

22 *Ibid.*, p. 52.

23 R. Barnes, *Mods!* London, Eel Pie, 1979, p. 10.

24 Tony, interviewed by the author, 1993.

25 J. Savage, 'Tainted Love: The Influence of Male Homosexuality and Sexual Divergence on Pop Music and Culture Since the War', in Alan Tomlinson (ed), *Consumption, Identity and Style: Marketing, Meanings and the Packaging of Pleasure*, London, Routledge, 1990, pp. 153–71.

26 P. Burton, *Parallel Lives*, London, GMP, 1985, pp. 30–1.

27 Q. Crisp, *The Naked Civil Servant*, London, Flamingo, 1985, p. 153.

28 BBC Radio programme 'Male Homosexual'. Broadcast 6 January 1964.

29 *Ibid.*

30 Brighton Ourstory Project, p. 51.

31 Cross-dressing has always played its part within the homosexual subculture. Oscar Wilde and his circle had frequented brothels where young male prostitutes wore women's clothes. For more information see R. Baker, *Drag*, London, Cassell 1994.

32 Hardy, interviewed, 1995.

33 Daniel, interviewed, 1997.

34 Brighton Ourstory Project, p. 56.

35 Hardy, interviewed, 1995.

36 Tony, interviewed, 1993.

37 Hardy, interviewed, 1995. The wearing of military uniforms, often in a civilian context, was another style of dress that became popular among gay men. For many these clothes were immediately available: they were doing or had done National Service and had kept hold of their uniforms. For others they offered a fantasy. Men in uniform were often the unavailable (or sometimes not so unavailable) object of men's sexual fantasy. There are a number of works which refer to the 'availability' of uniformed members of the armed forces for sexual liaisons, for example, Crisp, *Naked Civil Servant*. Dressing up could go some way to fulfilling that fantasy. Montague Glover's private photographs, published in 1992, show his lovers in a series of body-hugging uniforms.

38 Brighton Ourstory Project, p. 53.

39 Quoted in F. Chenoune, *A History of Men's Fashion*, Paris, Flammarion, 1993, p. 258.

40 Tony, interviewed, 1993.

41 *Ibid.*

42 For a detailed account of the 1967 Sexual Offences Act see part four of J. Weeks, *Coming Out: Homosexual Politics in Britain from the Nineteenth Century to the Present*, London, Quartet Books, 1990.

43 For personal accounts of the Stonewall riots see M. Duberman, *Stonewall*, New York, Plume, 1993.

44 Tony, interviewed, 1993.

Index